Contents

Helion & Company Limited
Unit 8 Amherst Business Centre, Budbrooke Road, Warwick CV34 5WE, England
Tel. 01926 499 619
Email: info@helion.co.uk Website: www.helion.co.uk Twitter: @helionbooks Visit our blog http://blog.helion.co.uk/

Published by Helion & Company 2026
Designed and typeset by Mach 3 Solutions (www.mach3solutions.co.uk)
Cover designed by Paul Hewitt, Battlefield Design (www.battlefield-design.co.uk)

Text © Martin Smisek 2026
Artworks © David Bocquelet & Tom Cooper 2026
Maps drawn by b.b.h.illustrations © Helion & Company 2026

ISBN 978-1-806720-28-6

British Library Cataloguing-in-Publication Data.
A catalogue record for this book is available from the British Library.

For details of other military history titles published by Helion & Company Limited contact the above address, or visit our website: http://www.helion.co.uk. We always welcome receiving book proposals from prospective authors.

ABBREVIATIONS AND ACRONYMS

AB	air base
ALN	*Armée de libération nationale* (National Liberation Army)
ANP	*Armée nationale populaire* (National Popular Army)
CSK	Czechoslovak koruna
DM	Deutsche Mark
FLN	*Front de libération nationale* (National Liberation Front)
FROLINAT	*Front de libération nationale du Tchad* (National Liberation Front of Chad)
GPRA	*Gouvernement provisoire de la République algérienne* (Provisional Government of the Algerian Republic)
HTS	*Hlavní technická správa* (Main Technical Administration)
KSČ	*Komunistická strana Československa* (Communist Party of Czechoslovakia)
LAAF	Libyan Arab Air Force
LF VAAZ	*Letecká fakulta Vojenské akademie Antonína Zápotockého* (Aviation Faculty of the Antonín Zápotocký Military Academy)
NATO	North Atlantic Treaty Organization
POLISARIO	*Popular de Liberación de Saguía el-Hamra y Río de Oro* (Popular Front for the Liberation of Saguia el-Hamra and Río de Oro)
RCC	Revolutionary Command Council
USD	US dollars
ÚV KSČ	*Ústřední výbor Komunistické strany Československa* (Central Committee of the Communist Party of Czechoslovakia)
VAAZ	*Vojenská akademie Antonína Zápotockého* (Antonín Zápotocký Military Academy)
ZF VAAZ	*Zahraniční fakulta Vojenské akademie Antonína Zápotockého* (Foreign Faculty of the Antonín Zápotocký Military Academy)

INTRODUCTION

After the end of the Second World War, the Czechoslovak arms industry tried to return to the significant position it had before the Nazi occupation of Czechoslovakia in March 1939. However, due to the onset of the Cold War, this was not entirely possible. The influence of the United States prevented Czechoslovak companies from exporting arms to Latin American countries. At the same time, Soviet dominance made it impossible to supply military hardware to the traditional Czechoslovak pre-war market in the Balkans. This left the Middle East as one of the few opportunities to build on the pre-war business.

Meanwhile, in the late 1940s, tensions in the area between Arabs and Jews began to escalate and eventually culminated in the 1948 Arab-Israeli War. Both sides tried to buy weapons around the world, including Czechoslovakia. In the same time frame, Czechoslovakia became an integral part of the Soviet Bloc which was foreshadowed by the communist coup d'état in February 1948. In the end, the Czechoslovak communist-led government decided, with backing from Moscow, to prefer the State of Israel in deliveries of armament. However, solid relations between Czechoslovakia and Israel were not to last forever. When it became clear that Israel would not become a communist country, Prague limited relations with the Jewish state. Moreover, in July 1950, the Czechoslovak Ministry of National Defence prohibited the export of all Czechoslovak weapons to Israel (more details about Czechoslovak arms deliveries to Israel can be found in Volume 1 of this series).

At the same time and in accordance with Soviet wishes, Prague embarked on the establishment of massive arms manufacturing capacities. The maximum weapons production between 1951 and 1953 was known as the three-year arms plan and was largely dedicated to the licensed production of Soviet guns, tanks and fighter aircraft, whose deliveries were then to be made primarily to the Czechoslovak army and other armed forces of the Soviet Bloc states. However, this policy ran into problems several years later when, due to the communist mismanagement and enormous arms spending, the recipient countries had problems buying additional weapons and paying for them.

At the same time, however, interest in the supply of armament from communist Czechoslovakia began to increase in Third World countries. Thanks to this, Prague was able to preserve its large capacity for the production of military hardware and earn the necessary foreign currency (Pounds sterling or the United States Dollar) by exporting weapons outside the Warsaw Pact states.

Syria became the first Arab nation to receive military hardware from a communist state in 1955, acquiring retired StuG III assault vehicles from Czechoslovakia. Nonetheless, the bulk of later shipments of Czechoslovak weaponry to Syria's armed forces were newly manufactured. Egypt soon followed, placing extensive orders for Czechoslovak armament also in 1955, sparking significant outrage and astonishment across the Western world. Several major arms agreements between Egypt and Czechoslovakia also included covert transfers of Soviet military gear. The weapon shipments were complemented by training programmes for Egyptian troops both in Czechoslovakia and within Egypt (specifics on the Czechoslovak arms exports and military assistance to Syria and Egypt are covered in Volumes 2 and 3 of this series). Amid these developments, the Mutawakkilite Kingdom of Yemen also expressed interest in Czechoslovak weaponry in 1956. The progression of events throughout the 1960s and 1970s paved the way for Prague to extend its military exports and assistance to Iraq, Iran, and South Yemen (these topics are explored in Volume 4 of this series).

Moreover, Czechoslovakia also delivered weapons and provided military assistance to Arab states in North Africa. While the very limited military relations between Czechoslovakia and Tunisia have already been described in the first volume of this series, this publication focuses on the deliveries of weapons and military hardware, as well as training provided to Algeria, Morocco, and the early years of the Czechoslovak military cooperation with Libya, up to 1979, with the remainder of that story to be told in Volume 6.

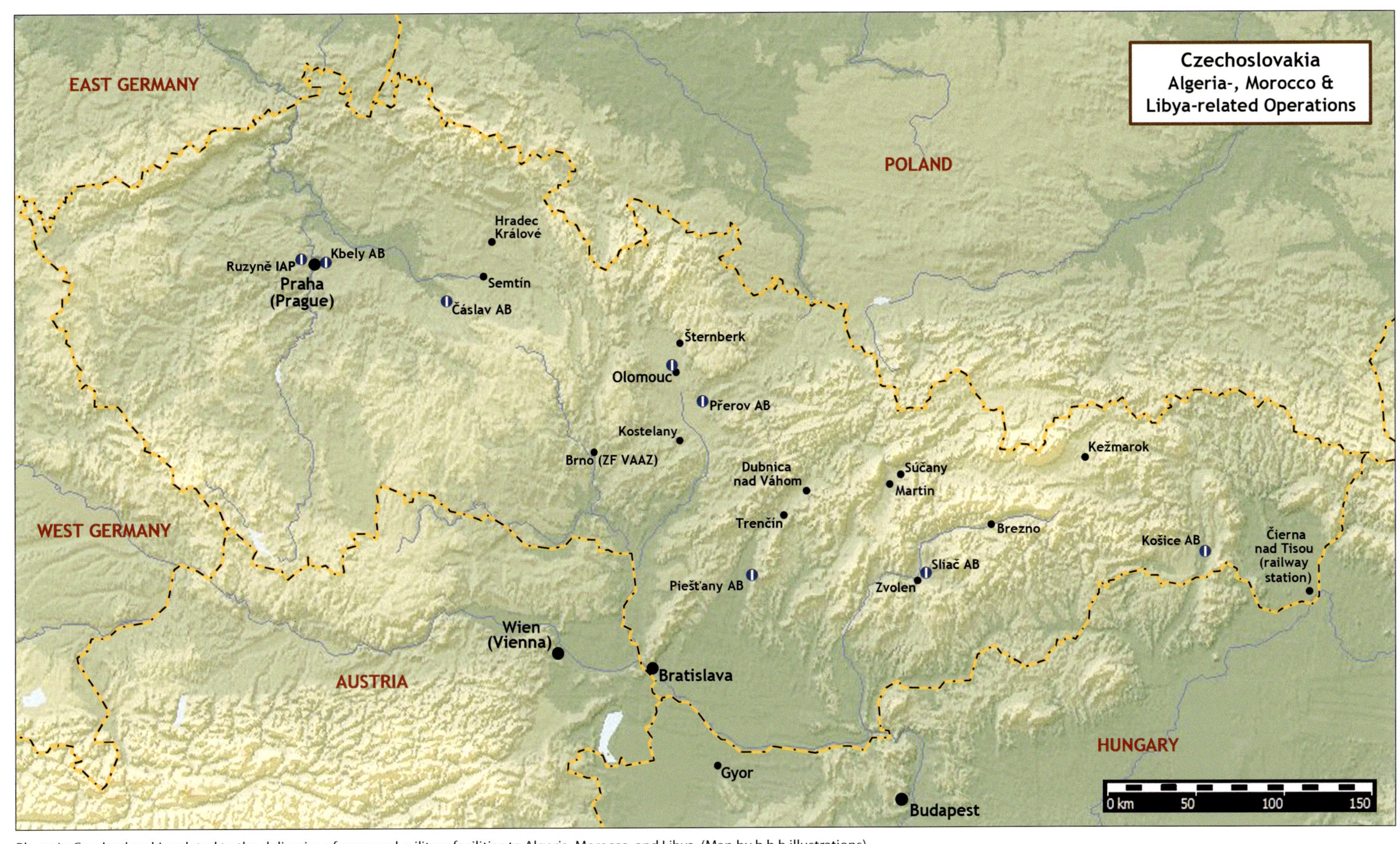

Places in Czechoslovakia related to the deliveries of arms and military facilities to Algeria, Morocco, and Libya. (Map by b.b.h.illustrations)

1

ALGERIA ('MOROCCO'/OPERATION 105C, 'MAURITANIA'/ OPERATION 130; COUNTRY 641)

After the Second World War, Czechoslovakia had its own diplomatic representation on Algerian soil (then colonial French Algeria), in the form of the consulate in Algiers, until May 1951. However, its further existence had to be terminated because respective French authorities did not issue an *exequatur* for the new Czechoslovak consul. At that time, the relations of Czechoslovak state officials in regard to French Algeria were limited only to representatives of the Algerian Communist Party. The situation changed after 1954 when the decolonisation war against the French authorities in Algeria, led primarily by the National Liberation Front (*Front de libération nationale*, FLN), started. In the beginning, Prague sided with the Algerian communists and ignored the FLN on the political and diplomatic landscape. This stance lasted some three years. Back then, the top-level officials of the Communist Party of Czechoslovakia (KSČ) decided to provide weapons for insurgents from the National Liberation Army (*Armée de libération nationale*, ALN), the armed wing of the FLN. It was the very first case in which communist Czechoslovakia delivered weapons to the rebels fighting the official government. However, the reasons were strictly commercial – shipments for the FLN enabled Prague to dispose of obsolete infantry armament in exchange for US dollars.

Initially, to obtain weapons was a great problem for the FLN. From 1955, the arms were smuggled from Egypt in caravans through Libya and Tunisia or with the assistance of small ships along the coast. From the insurgents' point of view, the situation improved dramatically in 1956 when France granted independence to Morocco and Tunisia. Both countries then started to carefully and discreetly support the FLN's cause.[1]

GUN TRAFFICKING

In January 1957, a Czechoslovak representative of the KOVO foreign trading company in Vienna was approached by Hamid Ouezzani, reportedly an Algerian doctor with a Moroccan passport, and Egyptian diplomat Ibrahim Mohammad Hassan, with a request for urgent acquisition of weapons from Czechoslovakia. As usual, the approval of Moscow was needed. The Soviets granted their permission for export of the weapons, but only on the condition that the arms would not be of Soviet origin, no matter if delivered to Czechoslovakia directly from the Soviet Union or manufactured under license in Czechoslovakia. The recipient country was officially stated as 'Morocco' and received the Czechoslovak codename Operation 105C. However, everybody involved was aware that the weapons were intended for the Algerian

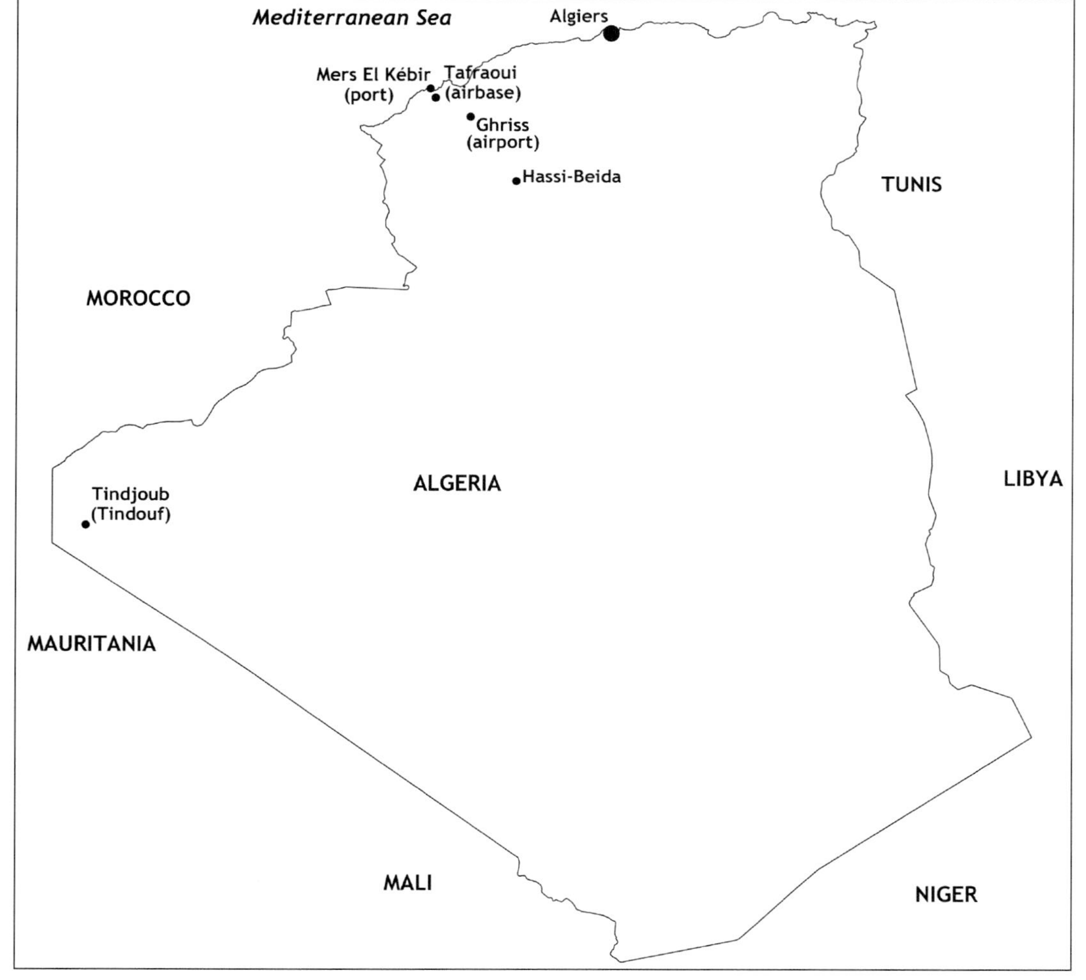

Map of places in Algeria mentioned in text and related to the deliveries of arms and military facilities, as well as the activity of the Czechoslovak military advisors and specialists. (Map by b.b.h.illustrations)

insurgents. Moreover, Hamid Ouezzani was, in fact, a *nom de guerre* of Driss Ben Said who acted as the main purchasing officer of the FLN in the Soviet Bloc countries.

He arrived in Czechoslovakia with the recommendation of Egyptian military attaché Farid in early February. On the 8th of the same month, Driss Ben Said attended a practical presentation of the offered weapons, mostly German types from the Second World War, and then discussed the details of the deal with the representatives of the Main Technical Administration (*Hlavní technická správa*, HTS) of the Ministry of Foreign Trade (*Ministerstvo zahraničního obchodu*), including its chief Major General František Macek. The Politburo (*Politické byro*) of the Central Committee of the Communist Party of Czechoslovakia (*Ústřední výbor Komunistické strany Československa*, ÚV KSČ) approved this undertaking as 'the deliveries of special material for an Egyptian company' on 26 February 1957. Correspondingly, Driss Ben Said then signed individual contracts for two shipments of hand grenades, pistols, rifles, submachine guns, machine guns, light anti-tank weapons, mortars, and related ammunition. With minor exceptions, it was generally captured armament of the German *Wehrmacht* that had been left behind on Czechoslovak territory after the end of the Second World War. The weapons ordered in the framework of the first deal (listed in Table 1) were dispatched from Czechoslovakia on 28 March 1957 and arrived in the Egyptian port of Alexandria without problems.[2]

Table 1: Operation 105C, the first shipment of arms, March 1957[3]

Type	Number of examples	Note
Radom, 9mm pistol	500	Czechoslovak designation of Polish VIS wz. 35, from the stocks of the Czechoslovak People's Army
vz. 38/40 N, 9mm submachine gun	3,000	Czechoslovak designation of German MP 38 and MP 40, delivered including spare parts, from the stocks of the Czechoslovak People's Army
vz. 98 N, 7.92mm rifle	6,000	Czechoslovak designation of German *Karabiner 98k*, delivered including spare parts, from the stocks of the Czechoslovak People's Army
vz. 34 N, 7.92mm machine gun	600	Czechoslovak designation of German MG 34, delivered including spare parts, from the stocks of the Czechoslovak People's Army
vz. 42 N, 7.92mm machine gun	500	Czechoslovak designation of German MG 42, delivered including spare parts, from the stocks of the Czechoslovak People's Army
vz. 48, 9mm round	5,000,000	from the stocks of the Czechoslovak People's Army
vz. 47, 7.92mm round	10,000,000	from the stocks of the Czechoslovak People's Army
vz. 34, hand grenade	30,000	from the stocks of the Czechoslovak People's Army
vz. 34 N, 82mm mortar	100	German *Granatwerfer 34* adapted in Czechoslovakia for Soviet 82mm shell, delivered including spare parts, from the stocks of the Czechoslovak People's Army
82-EO-čs-bz-M, 82mm high explosive mortar round	20,000	from the stocks of the Czechoslovak People's Army

The second contract was arranged with the assistance of the Swiss company Félix et Cie playing the role of the middleman that sold the weapons (listed in Table 2) officially only from Czechoslovakia to Yugoslavia as a final user state (the alleged recipient of the armament is quoted as Mauritania in the official documentation of Czechoslovak Ministry of National Defence). However, in the Yugoslavian port of Bakar, the arms were loaded on the ship *Srbija* that transported them to the Moroccan port of Casablanca in August 1957. The weapons were formally seized by Moroccan Police and subsequently handed over to the 'right' recipient.[4]

Table 2: Operation 105C, the second shipment of arms (for 'Mauritania'), May 1957[5]

Type	Number of examples	Note
vz. 98 N, 7.92mm rifle	2,000	Czechoslovak designation of German *Karabiner 98k*, delivered including spare parts, from the stocks of the Czechoslovak People's Army
vz. 42 N, 7.92mm machine gun	50	Czechoslovak designation of German MG 42, delivered including spare parts, from the stocks of the Czechoslovak People's Army
vz. 38/46, 12.7mm anti-aircraft machine gun	13	Czechoslovak license of Soviet DShKM, delivered including spare parts, from the stocks of the Czechoslovak People's Army
P-27, light anti-tank weapon	20	delivered including spare parts, from the stocks of the Czechoslovak People's Army
vz. 47, 7.92mm round	2,000,000	from the stocks of the Czechoslovak People's Army
12,7-PZ, 12.7mm armour-piercing incendiary round	2,400	from the stocks of the Czechoslovak People's Army
12,7-PZSv, 12.7mm armour-piercing incendiary round with tracer	300	from the stocks of the Czechoslovak People's Army
round for P-27	364	from the stocks of the Czechoslovak People's Army

Due to the need to maintain secrecy, Ben Said's last deal with the Czechoslovak authorities in 1957 was concluded in the form of two signed delivery specifications only. Again, the company Félix et Cie acted as the middleman and handed over to the Czechoslovak consul in Switzerland a sum worth 262,000 USD in cash. Despite the insistence on the utmost secrecy of the deliveries, the recklessness of

Czechoslovak officials responsible for the railway transport resulted in a major international scandal. The weapons and ammunition (listed in Table 3) from various military warehouses filled one train composed of 14 railway cars that was dispatched from Bratislava-Petržalka railway station in December 1957. Driving through Hungary, the train arrived in the Yugoslav port of Bakar where its cargo was transferred aboard the Yugoslav ship *Slovenija*. Although all signs and symbols showing Czechoslovak origin were to be removed from all the arms, ammunition, and their crates, no one issued an order that would prohibit the placement of transport documentation, containing information about the delivery and supplying warehouse, into the crates. Moreover, the accompanying cargo documents, which were freely accessible to a wide number of railway workers in Hungary and Yugoslavia, stated openly that the train was transporting armament.

Soldiers of the 9th Parachute Chasseur Regiment with captured Algerian insurgents and a vz. 42 N (MG 42) machine gun. (via Martin Smisek)

A vz. 34 N mortar, from a shipment impounded aboard the Yugoslav ship *Slovenija*. (via Martin Smisek)

However, the French intelligence services got wind about these developments, including the dubious activities of Ben Said in Prague, and on 8 January 1958, informed respective French institutions about the imminent arrival of *Slovenija* into Casablanca. Therefore, two French destroyers, *Cassard* and *Kabyle*, intercepted the Yugoslav vessel 45 nautical miles off the Algerian coast on Saturday, 18 January 1958, and escorted it into Oran, a coastal city located in the north-west of Algeria. In a major success, French authorities confiscated the whole cargo of some 150 tonnes that could equip 6,000 insurgents for three months. Hence, a large part of the Czechoslovak supply was lost. The French captured 1,500 pistols, 1,000 submachine guns, 4,000 rifles, 200 machine guns, 10 mortars with 6,000 shells, 48 light anti-tank weapons with 2,000 rounds of ammunition, 300 linear charges, and 2 million rounds of 7.92mm ammunition. This affair represented a major Czechoslovak fiasco on the international scene. Transport documentation from the warehouse at Bílek was left in one of the crates and Czechoslovak insignia was removed only sloppily from the arms. Thus, the original source of the weapons became more than clear and Prague duly became the target of French diplomatic protests and negative public attention as the Czechoslovak enterprise was described in the French newspaper *Le Figaro* on 31 January 1958.[6]

Table 3: Operation 105C, the third shipment of arms, December 1957[7]

Type	Number of examples	Note
vz. 24, 9mm pistol	3,000	from the stocks of the Czechoslovak People's Army
vz. 98 N, 7.92mm rifle	6,000	Czechoslovak designation of German *Karabiner 98k*, delivered including spare parts, from the stocks of the Czechoslovak People's Army
vz. 34 N, 7.92mm machine gun	100	Czechoslovak designation of German MG 34, delivered including spare parts, from the stocks of the Czechoslovak People's Army
vz. 42 N, 7.92mm machine gun	354	Czechoslovak designation of German MG 42, delivered including spare parts, from the stocks of the Czechoslovak People's Army
9mm round	550,000	for vz. 24 pistol, from the stocks of the Czechoslovak People's Army
vz. 48, 9mm round	200,000	from the stocks of the Czechoslovak People's Army
vz. 47, 7.92mm round	7,000,000	from the stocks of the Czechoslovak People's Army
P-27, light anti-tank weapon	48	delivered including spare parts, from the stocks of the Czechoslovak People's Army
round for P-27	2,000	from the stocks of the Czechoslovak People's Army
vz. 34 N, 82mm mortar	10	German *Granatwerfer 34* adapted in Czechoslovakia for Soviet 82mm shell, delivered including spare parts, from the stocks of the Czechoslovak People's Army

Vz. 34 N mortars of the ALN, seen in around 1960. (via Martin Smisek)

82-EO-čs-bz-M, 82mm high explosive mortar round	6,000	from the stocks of the Czechoslovak People's Army
TN, linear charge (1.5 meters)	330	from the stocks of the Czechoslovak People's Army

Vz 98 N rifles from Czechoslovakia, as found aboard *Slovenija*. (via Martin Smisek)

DELIVERY FOR THE ROYAL MOROCCAN ARMY

However, international embarrassment did not discourage Prague from further deliveries of weapons to Morocco. Between 29 August and 3 September 1958, a Moroccan delegation composed of the director of the Economic Department of the Ministry of Foreign Affairs, Ben Jelloun, and the representative of the Ministry of National Defence, Mr. Bouchamin, visited Czechoslovakia in order to discuss deliveries of infantry weapons and Czechoslovak preparedness to build an ammunition plant in Morocco and to produce 7.5mm rounds according to the Moroccan documentation in Czechoslovakia. This time, Moroccan officials assured their Czechoslovak counterparts that the arms in question would be intended strictly for the Royal Moroccan Army.

The Politburo ÚV KSČ approved the delivery of captured German arms on 2 September. After obligatory consultation with Moscow, the Soviets in an aide-mémoire from 23 October informed Prague that they had no objections to delivery of 'non-Soviet types' of weapons, the establishment of an ammunition plant in Morocco, and production of 7.5mm rounds for the Moroccan armed forces.

Other weaponry of Czechoslovak origin sent to the ALN, but captured aboard *Slovenija*. (via Martin Smisek)

Therefore, the Politburo ÚV KSČ duly decided to satisfy all Moroccan arms demands worth 802,000 GBP (16.2 million CSK) in its further resolution on 4 November. The only problem arose in the case of the requested number of submachine guns that had to be scaled down to 3,000 examples from the original demand of 12,000 – such quantity of German weapons of this type was not available in the warehouses of the Czechoslovak People's Army (*Československá lidová armáda*). After the previous negative experience with Yugoslavia, the HTS initially insisted that the Moroccans secure the transport of the weapons to Casablanca on their own. However, Moroccan officials expressed their inability to arrange such an operation. Following some hesitation, Prague decided to accept the Moroccan appeals and organise delivery of the weapons as this was an official deal between both governments.

The weapons, officially for Morocco (listed in Table 4), were dispatched from Czechoslovakia on 17 December 1958 and supplied to the Polish port of Gdynia. All Czech texts, insignias, markings, and documents were removed from the packages. In Poland, the armament and ammunition weighing 900 tonnes were embarked on the merchant ship *Mönkedamm*, of a West German shipping company, and transported flawlessly to Casablanca on 2 January 1959. In the end, the remaining parts of the resolution from 4 November – the establishment of an ammunition factory in Morocco and production of 7.5mm rounds in Czechoslovakia – did not come to be. As of late 1967, the whole Moroccan arms industry was composed of a single small plant near Fez which produced ammunition and assembled pistols, submachine guns, and light machine guns. The facility was equipped exclusively with Italian production machinery.[8]

Table 4: Operation 105C, the fourth shipment of arms, December 1958[9]

Type	Number of examples	Note
vz. 27, 7.65mm pistol	501	from the stocks of the Czechoslovak People's Army
vz. 38/40 N, 9mm submachine gun	3,000	Czechoslovak designation of German MP 38 and MP 40, delivered including spare parts, from the stocks of the Czechoslovak People's Army
vz. 43 N, 7.92mm rifle	2,000	Czechoslovak designation of German *Gewehr 43*, delivered including spare parts, from the stocks of the Czechoslovak People's Army
vz. 48, 9mm round	30,009,600	from the stocks of the Czechoslovak People's Army
vz. 47, 7.92mm round	1,003,500	from the stocks of the Czechoslovak People's Army
RG-4, hand grenade	50,600	from the stocks of the Czechoslovak People's Army
vz. 42 N, 120mm mortar	6	Czechoslovak designation of German *Granatwerfer 42*, delivered including spare parts, from the stocks of the Czechoslovak People's Army
120mm high explosive mortar round	12,000	from the stocks of the Czechoslovak People's Army
PP-Mi D, wooden anti-personnel mine	52,000	from the stocks of the Czechoslovak People's Army
PT-TO-Mi Ba, bakelite anti-tank mine	5,000	from the stocks of the Czechoslovak People's Army

THE *LIDICE* AFFAIR

On 14 November 1958, the Politburo ÚV KSČ occupied itself with one more arms deal related to Morocco. Although originally this one was not so straightforward, the enterprise was approved without objections. Vimmer Lanquet, the representative of the company Nawiland Trust from Vaduz in Liechtenstein, visited the director of the HTS, Major General František Macek, on 22 October 1958 with a request for the delivery of 2,000 MG 42 machine guns, 1,000 spare barrels for the MG 42, 5,000 *Karabiner 98k* rifles, and 10 million rounds of 7.92mm ammunition. According to his statement, the weapons and ammunition in question were intended for Morocco only. As proof of this intention, he submitted a copy of the contract between Nawiland and officials of Tanger (Tangier) province from 24 September 1958 and a declaration of provincial governor Dr. Abdellatif Ben Jelloun from the same day. However, the official report for the Politburo ÚV KSČ added that 'with regard to the nature of the delivery and the political situation, the Moroccan government cannot conduct this transaction directly and is therefore carried out by government posts at Tanger'. Although Lanquet served as a middleman during the previous shipment of arms on board *Mönkedamm*, he was excluded from further negotiations in February 1959 due to his 'unsatisfactory payment conditions'. Therefore, subsequent talks were led directly between the HTS (under the disguise of foreign trading company OMNIPOL) and the Moroccan Ministry of National Defence. They culminated with the signing of a contract worth 1,632,000 USD (11.750 million CSK) on 16 March 1959 (the weapons and ammunition purchased are listed in Table 5). Satisfaction with this good business was not to last long because a subsequent series of minor and larger mistakes made by various Czechoslovak officials led to a diplomatic disaster caused by French interception of the Czechoslovak merchant ship *Lidice* loaded full of weapons.

Table 5: Operation 105C, the fifth shipment of arms (captured on the ship *Lidice*), March 1959[10]

Type	Number of examples	Note
vz. 98 N, 7.92mm rifle	12,000	Czechoslovak designation of German *Karabiner 98k*, delivered including spare parts, from the stocks of the Czechoslovak People's Army
vz. 42 N, 7.92mm machine gun	2,000	Czechoslovak designation of German MG 42, delivered including spare parts and 2,000 replacement barrels, from the stocks of the Czechoslovak People's Army
vz. 48, 9mm round	2,000,000	from the stocks of the Czechoslovak People's Army
vz. 47, 7.92mm round	10,000,000	from the stocks of the Czechoslovak People's Army

In order to save hard currency, which was at a premium in communist Czechoslovakia, František Nový, an official of the Czechoslovak shipping company Čechofracht that was responsible for the delivery of the 'special cargo' to Morocco, decided to use the Czechoslovak ship *Lidice* and not a vessel from some 'non-participating' West European country, as in the case of *Mönkedamm* for the previous shipment. Moreover, he chose a shorter route which saved one day of travel. Thus, the ship did not circumnavigate Denmark but went through the Kiel Canal. More importantly, a formal customs inspection was undertaken here and in order to maintain the secrecy of the delivery, cover documents describing the load as a general cargo for the Democratic Republic of Vietnam were prepared and subsequently presented in West Germany. However, this violated two international conventions at the same time. Firstly, it was prohibited to declare ammunition and explosives as general cargo and secondly, deliveries of military materiel to North Vietnam were not allowed at that time.

This, in turn, meant that Ladislav Makový, the skipper of *Lidice*, had two sets of documents, the genuine one listing the weapons with the destination of Casablanca, and the other fabricated quoting Haiphong as the port of the recipient country. Because of poor communication, Makový was not thoroughly briefed on how to use these documents properly. He was left with the impression that the authentic documentation could be used only in the port of Casablanca. The ship *Lidice* was loaded from 37 railway cars in the Polish port Gdynia between 25 and 28 March 1959. Despite the sensitivity of the cargo, absolutely no security measures were taken here in order to ensure the secrecy of the enterprise.

The vessel left Poland on 28 March and it fell behind schedule shortly thereafter because of the fog in front of the Kiel Canal and subsequent breakdown of its refrigerating equipment. Due to an incorrectly understood telegram, the repair of the ship took longer than expected which resulted in anchoring in Kiel harbour for 56 hours. In the meantime, the French authorities got wind of the operation and were taking steps to prevent *Lidice* from accomplishing its mission. However, nothing was lost yet as Moroccan informants found out that the French Navy had dispatched its ships with the task of intercepting the Czechoslovak merchant vessel. Wasting no time, the Moroccan government in its special meeting, on Sunday 5 April, decided to pre-empt French action with the public announcement that the Czechoslovak ship *Lidice* transporting weapons and ammunition for the Royal Moroccan Army was awaited at Casablanca. The news was picked up by French press agency AFP on the next day and the Parisian newspaper *Le Monde* published a related account on 7 April. Although HTS representative Josef Knytl, who was awaiting the arrival of *Lidice* in Morocco, was informed about the pronouncement of the Moroccan government without delay, inadequate communication and coordination on the part of various Czechoslovak institutions meant that respective officials at the Ministry of Foreign Trade and Ministry of Foreign Affairs (*Ministerstvo zahraničních věcí*) were not informed about the situation appropriately and therefore could not actively take corrective action. Moreover, the skipper Makový never received a warning about imminent danger or instruction on how to react to the French inspection of *Lidice*. Thus, the die was cast.

On 6 April 1959, a couple of minutes before 6:00 a.m., the Czechoslovak ship was caught by the frigate *Le Bearnais* (F 775) of the French Navy just 20 nautical miles off Casablanca. The frigate came closer and, at 6:14 a.m., issued a signal to *Lidice* ordering it to stop. At first, the Czechoslovak skipper ignored the order, but the French vessel fired a dummy round in front of *Lidice* which

The freighter *Lidice* seen after being impounded. (via Martin Smisek)

A view into the cargo hold of the freighter *Lidice*, full of wooden crates with arms and ammunition. (via Martin Smisek)

A crate with vz. 98 N 7.92mm rifles, found aboard the freighter *Lidice*. (via Martin Smisek)

prompted Ladislav Makový to stop immediately at 6:18 a.m. At 6:45 a.m. *Le Bearnais* was joined by a second Le Normand-class frigate of the French Navy – *Le Basque* (F 773). In the meantime, *Le Bearnais* sent a motorboat towards the Czechoslovak ship with eight sailors and two officers who boarded *Lidice* at 6:50 a.m. Although Makový had time to establish contact with a radio station at Szczecin and informed them about the developing situation, he did nothing. Therefore, the Czechoslovak authorities were left in the dark about the beginning of the incident which the communist leadership in Prague called later a blatant act of piracy.

Upon an order from one of the French officers, the Czechoslovak skipper presented the fabricated documents showing Haiphong as the destination of the vessel. This sparked great interest on the French side and Makový had to explain why the ship was near Casablanca and not at Port Said when the vessel should be on its way to South East Asia. He invented an excuse that he received a radiotelegram from Prague with an order to change heading to Casablanca and to wait there for further instructions. Makový even presented a hastily fabricated document to support his statement while he managed to destroy the original ones. French officers remained unconvinced and thus *Lidice* was escorted by both frigates to the Algerian port of Mers El Kébir near Oran where it anchored around 11:00 a.m. on 8 April.

Not able to establish contact with the vessel, some Czechoslovak officials began to worry about the fate of the ship which was in the process of being thoroughly inspected in the ample presence of journalists. The French authorities took only a little time to discover that the alleged 'general cargo' for the Democratic Republic of Vietnam was composed of a large number of infantry weapons and related ammunition. While Moroccan diplomatic officials were doing their best to save the situation, their counterparts from Prague were just getting a grasp of the gravity of the circumstances. The Czechoslovak tragicomedy of errors culminated in a protest note which was readied only on 10 April and which contained a statement that all documentation on board *Lidice* was correct – the officials who were preparing the note were not informed about the fact that the relevant documents, which remained on the ship at the time of its arrival in Mers El Kébir, were only those that had been fabricated. After unloading and confiscating the entire cargo of 3,996 crates with a weight of more than 580 tonnes, the ship was released on 12 April 1959 at 0:15 a.m. The scandal strained Czechoslovak-French relations for several subsequent years.[11]

AFTERMATH

Representing a fiasco of major proportions, the *Lidice* scandal had far-reaching consequences in Czechoslovakia. A resolution was accepted that forbade the transport of weapons aboard Czechoslovak ships excluding those that received expressed permission of the Politburo ÚV KSČ. The director of the HTS, Major General František Macek, was removed from his office on 26 May 1959 and transferred back to the Czechoslovak People's Army. In his post was appointed František Mareš, then director of the foreign trading company Chemapol. Several officials from the Čechofracht shipping company were dismissed, reprimanded, or demoted to less responsible duties. The HTS itself underwent a thorough inspection which showed a disproportionately high number of its workers had low knowledge of trade issues.

Although Rabat requested the return of the captured weapons, the Moroccans were unsuccessful because the appropriate documentation on board *Lidice* had been destroyed by its skipper. The French authorities argued that no evidence was found that could support Moroccan claims as the ship transported 'old German weapons with removed insignia' only. Enraged, Moroccan officials declared that the *Lidice* affair was a matter between France and Czechoslovakia and Minister of Defence Aouad demanded a replacement delivery which would compensate for the loss caused by the French seizure of the cargo of *Lidice*. Czechoslovak officials consulted upon the question with Moscow and Soviet representatives took a positive stand on the new delivery of captured German weaponry to Morocco. Subsequently, the Politburo ÚV KSČ approved the substitute supply on 28 July 1959 but only on the condition that Moroccan authorities would arrange transportation of the cargo to Casablanca at their own risk. This was apparently one of the reasons that ultimately stalled the delivery and thus Rabat received no replacement for the weapons captured by the French. Moreover, the *Lidice* affair represented a major diplomatic fiasco for Prague and this, in turn, completely discouraged the Czechoslovak communists from further shipments of arms for the FLN through Morocco.[12]

SOVIET ASSISTANCE

The next round of supplies from the warehouses of the Czechoslovak People's Army for the FLN was related to the delivery of an engine and spare parts for the C-47 Skytrain transport aircraft which were dispatched from Czechoslovakia between October and December 1960.[13]

Due to the previous embarrassing developments, new deliveries of arms for the ALN were discussed directly with the Provisional Government of the Algerian Republic (*Gouvernement provisoire de*

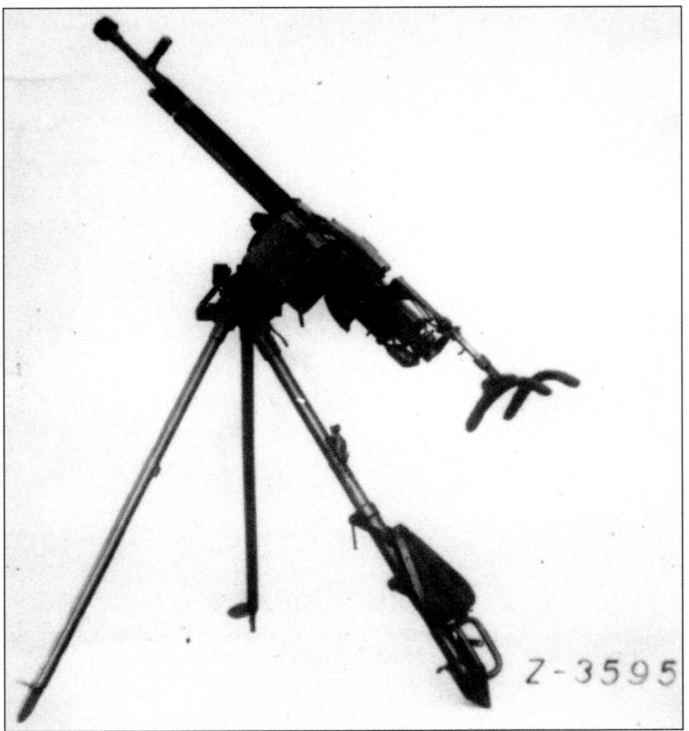

A vz. 38/46 12.7mm heavy machine gun. (VÚA-VHA Praha)

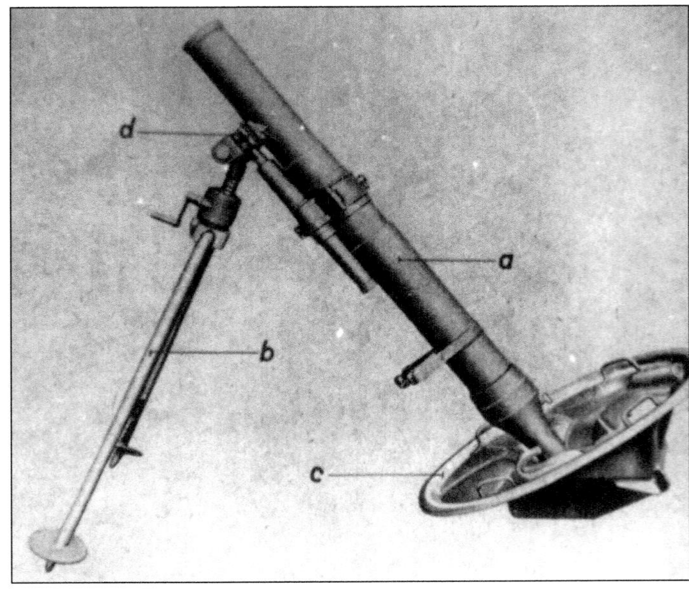

A vz. 42 N 120mm mortar. (VÚA-VHA Praha)

la République algérienne, GPRA) which was set up in Cairo on 19 September 1958. Algerian Minister of Economy and Finance Ahmed Francis and Secretary of the Ministry of Foreign Affairs Saad Dahlab were staying in Prague between 7 and 10 February 1961. During negotiations with various Czechoslovak officials, they requested a free of charge supply of food, clothes, medicaments, vehicles, and other goods. Therefore, the Politburo ÚV KSČ granted its approval for the supply of civilian items on 14 February 1961 and the corresponding protocol was signed on 25 March 1961 which, from the Czechoslovak side, served as a *de facto* recognition of the GPRA. Although officially declared as civilian deliveries, they included not only medicaments, 1,000 tonnes of sugar, 40,000 tonnes of soap, 30,000kg of condensed milk, tents, 20,000 blouses, seven Zetor Super tractors, 30 JAWA 350 motorcycles, and 20 Praga V3S trucks, but 500 military tents and parts of uniforms such as 10,000 coats, 30,000 service shirts, 10,000 cotton pants with the same number of belts, and 30,000 pocket bandages as well.

However, the military materiel from this donation was provided as part of a subsequent 'special' delivery (Table 6) which was also discussed with Ahmed Francis and Saad Dahlab during their Prague stay in February. Algerian representatives placed the greatest emphasis on the provision of weapons during meetings with Czechoslovak officials. Because Soviet agreement for such undertaking was needed, an aide-mémoire requesting the approval of the deal and outlining the terms of delivery was handed over to the Soviet Ambassador in Prague, Zimyanin, on 23 February. The affirmative reply arrived on 20 March and the matter was discussed, among other topics, in Moscow around the same time frame between the HTS director František Mareš and his Soviet counterpart – deputy chairman of the State Committee for Foreign Economic Relations Lieutenant General Georgy Stepanovich Sidorovich. The Soviets were delighted and approved all Czechoslovak points.

The transport of weapons would follow the pattern which had already been used for arms shipments from the Soviet Union and the People's Republic of China for the ALN for some time. This method used the United Arab Republic as a place for the transshipment. All needed details related to the deliveries were discussed between the representatives of the GPRA and Egyptian officials only. Then, Moscow supplied the weapons to the port in Alexandria without any written documentation. After some time, in order to check whether everything went flawlessly, Soviet officials asked the Algerians if the shipment had been handed over to them. In this way, Moscow delivered (or planned to deliver) infantry weapons, vehicles, medical material, mobile printing machine, 82mm and 120mm mortars, 85mm field guns, 122mm howitzers, ammunition, and related spare parts. As the stocks of captured German weaponry were already depleted, Moscow provided armament of Soviet origin from the times of the Second World War. After receiving a positive reply from the Soviet Union, the Politburo ÚV KSČ approved the delivery of mostly surplus weapons and ammunition together with combat clothing and personal equipment (listed in Table 6) to the value of 38.2 million CSK on 28 March 1961. No written contract was signed between the Czechoslovak government and GPRA. Prague used this opportunity to dispose of the oldest stocks in its military warehouses. Despite its age, all armament was provided in combat-ready condition. Military cooperation with the GPRA received the Czechoslovak cover name Operation 130 (however, in order to maintain the secrecy, the country related to this designation was still listed as Morocco in Czechoslovak official documentation).[14]

Table 6: Operation 130, delivery of military materiel for the GPRA, May/June 1961[15]

Type	Number of examples	Note
vz. 44, 26.5mm signal pistol	50	from the stocks of the Czechoslovak People's Army
26.5mm signal round	4,500	from the stocks of the Czechoslovak People's Army
vz. 27, 7.65mm pistol	2,000	from the stocks of the Czechoslovak People's Army
vz. 98 N, 7.92mm rifle	8,000	Czechoslovak designation of German *Karabiner 98k*, from the stocks of the Czechoslovak People's Army
vz. 34 N, 7.92mm machine gun	1,000	Czechoslovak designation of German MG 34, from the stocks of the Czechoslovak People's Army
vz. 43, 7.62mm machine gun	250	the Czechoslovak license of SG-43, from the stocks of the Czechoslovak People's Army
7.62mm rimfire round	2,000,000	from the stocks of the Czechoslovak People's Army
7.65mm pistol round	240,000	from the stocks of the Czechoslovak People's Army
vz. 47, 7.92mm round	10,000,000	from the stocks of the Czechoslovak People's Army
RG-4, hand grenade	200,000	from the stocks of the Czechoslovak People's Army
P-27, light anti-tank weapon	100	from the stocks of the Czechoslovak People's Army
round for P-27	1,000	from the stocks of the Czechoslovak People's Army
vz. 41 S, 82mm mortar	200	Czechoslovak designation of Soviet M1941, from the stocks of the Czechoslovak People's Army
vz. 24, 120mm mortar	100	from the stocks of the Czechoslovak People's Army
82mm fragmentation mortar round	100,000	from the stocks of the Czechoslovak People's Army
120mm high explosive mortar round	40,000	from the stocks of the Czechoslovak People's Army
vz. 42 S, 76mm gun	18	Czechoslovak designation of Soviet M1942 (ZiS-3), from the stocks of the Czechoslovak People's Army
vz. 18/40 N, 105mm howitzer	18	Czechoslovak designation of German *10,5 cm leichte Feldhaubitze 18*, from the stocks of the Czechoslovak People's Army
76mm fragmentation round	8,400	from the stocks of the Czechoslovak People's Army
76mm armour-piercing round	4,200	from the stocks of the Czechoslovak People's Army

105mm high explosive round	7,200	from the stocks of the Czechoslovak People's Army
different artillery optical and measuring equipment	-	from the stocks of the Czechoslovak People's Army
PT-Mi D, wooden anti-tank mine	20,000	from the stocks of the Czechoslovak People's Army
vz. 53, tent for 10 persons	500	from the stocks of the Czechoslovak People's Army
čepice bavlněná 21, cotton cap	10,000	from the stocks of the Czechoslovak People's Army
čepice soukenná 21, cloth cap	10,000	from the stocks of the Czechoslovak People's Army
kalhoty bavlněné 21, cotton pants	10,000	from the stocks of the Czechoslovak People's Army
blůza soukenná 21, cloth field jacket	10,000	from the stocks of the Czechoslovak People's Army

plášť soukenný 21, cloth coat	10,000	from the stocks of the Czechoslovak People's Army
košile 21, service shirt	30,000	from the stocks of the Czechoslovak People's Army
tílko 25, undershirt	20,000	from the stocks of the Czechoslovak People's Army
summer underpants	20,000	from the stocks of the Czechoslovak People's Army
vz. 30, rucksack	10,000	from the stocks of the Czechoslovak People's Army
vz. 30, pouch	10,000	from the stocks of the Czechoslovak People's Army
leather belt	10,000	from the stocks of the Czechoslovak People's Army
flask	10,000	from the stocks of the Czechoslovak People's Army
pláštěnka stanová 53, poncho	20,000	with pegs and supports, from the stocks of the Czechoslovak People's Army
leather strap	30,000	from the stocks of the Czechoslovak People's Army
low shoes	10,000	from the stocks of the Czechoslovak People's Army
pocket bandages	30,000	from the stocks of the Czechoslovak People's Army

The materiel was dispatched in two consignments between 28 May and 1 June 1961. At the request of Algerian representatives, the uniforms and other personal equipment was supplied by Czechoslovak shipping company Metrans as civilian cargo to Tunisia. The weapons and ammunition were loaded on 224 railway cars and transported in 19 trains to Čierna nad Tisou on the Czechoslovak-Soviet (today Slovak-Ukrainian) border. There, Czechoslovak soldiers transferred the cargo onto Soviet railway cars which ferried them to the port for shipment aboard a merchant ship. The Soviets delivered the freight from Czechoslovakia to Alexandria free of charge. The delivery of armament and ammunition was coordinated with the United Arab Republic, thus the only person responsible for the handover of Czechoslovak arms representing the customer was an Egyptian official, Colonel Rahmy. All delivered materiel was disembarked in Alexandria without any complications between 23 and 28 June 1961. The weapons and ammunition were then loaded on trucks and transported through Libya to the hands of respective Algerian officials.[16]

The MG 34 7.92mm machine gun was manufactured on Czechoslovak territory during the Second World War at Waffenwerke Brünn (Zbrojovka Brno). After the conflict, captured weapons were used by the Czechoslovak army under the designation vz. 34 N. (VÚA-VHA Praha)

TRAINING, RE-EXPORT, AND SABOTAGE

Unlike previous instances, this time Prague provided a crash course at the Foreign Faculty of the Antonín Zápotocký Military Academy in Brno on the operation of the delivered artillery weapons for selected members of the ALN. Four Algerians (Hocine Benmaalan, Ahmed Hamadi, Abdelmalez Cuenaiza, and Mohamed Tonati) arrived in Czechoslovakia on 3 May 1961. According to the original plan, the training was to take place for two months. However, after information from the business attaché in Cairo, it had to be shortened to just four weeks. With such a limited amount of time, the instruction aimed to acquaint the Algerians with the technical basics of the supplied guns and then to teach them how to undertake simple firing missions. After graduating from the course, all four were to be ready to serve as instructors who would train further troops of the ALN. Actual training started on 10 May with six to eight training hours per day. From the third week, the tempo was increased to 10 training hours a day, which placed great demands not only on the students but the Czechoslovak instructors and interpreters as well. Training of the Algerians was concluded with a live firing exercise which served as a verification of their newly attained skills in the practical operation of the guns and their knowledge of how to control the fire of an artillery platoon and battery. The Algerian students worked hard and thus their training was finished successfully on 10 June 1961. They left Czechoslovakia three days later.[17]

Not all Czechoslovak weapons for the Algerian insurgents were delivered directly from Czechoslovakia. L Kyuchkov, the director of the Engineering Administration of the Bulgarian Ministry of Foreign Trade, turned to his Czechoslovak counterpart at the HTS, František Mareš, in a letter from 11 May 1961 in which he asked for the delivery of 35,000 rounds for the P-27 light anti-tank weapon. This ammunition, to the value of some 3.7 million CSK, was to be subsequently provided to the GPRA using credit. The Bulgarians demanded an early date of delivery. Since these rounds were not in production, the Czechoslovak Ministry of National Defence (*Ministerstvo národní obrany*) gave its consent to supply the requested ammunition from the stocks of the Czechoslovak People's Army. At the same time, Bulgarian officials made a promise that all Czechoslovak marking would be removed from the ammunition and its transport boxes in order to conceal the true source of the delivery. The Politburo ÚV KSČ duly approved the deal in a resolution of 13 June 1961. All rounds were sent off to the People's Republic of Bulgaria in two train transports during July 1961.

However, this undertaking raised some suspicion in Prague. Some officials assumed that Bulgaria could plan to deliver the P-27 light anti-tank weapons as well (the Bulgarian People's Army obtained 1,050 of them during the early 1950s). Alternatively, the weapons could have already been provided by another country. In both cases, it would be a violation of respective arms agreements as Prague always insisted on its permission if some Czechoslovak weapon should be re-exported. In the end, Czechoslovak officials decided not to press this issue further because the investigation could be 'very difficult and apparently inappropriate as well'.[18]

It would appear that the French intelligence services got wind about some of the Czechoslovak deliveries and took appropriate measures. Therefore, a Czechoslovak technician, Blažek, working for the Tunisian Ministry of Public Works at Kef was approached by Algerian officials with a request for help in January 1962. Kef was an important logistic hub for the ALN and in recent days 10 new Praga V3S military trucks had been delivered there (probably through Libya as part of Operation 15). The Algerians claimed that they had some technical difficulties with the trucks and asked Blažek if he could check the technical condition of the vehicles. Blažek complied with the Algerians' wishes and after an inspection, he found out that four trucks had arrived without the nuts in their steering system. Being considered as sabotage, he immediately informed the respective official at the Czechoslovak embassy in Tunisia on 20 January. During the same day, a dispatch was sent to Prague with a request to check, as a precaution, an additional 30 Praga V3S trucks that were just being readied for delivery to the ALN.[19]

AIRCRAFT TECHNICIANS

The bloody guerrilla war against French rule continued until 18 March 1962 when both warring parties reached an agreement by signing the Evian Accords. A ceasefire was proclaimed from that day onwards, and France agreed to the self-determination of Algeria. Full independence was granted following a referendum on 1 July 1962 in which the vote was nearly unanimous for an independent Algeria. During the last quarter of the same year, Prague delivered various medical supplies to the overall value of 1,498,000 CSK.[20]

Commemorating the first successfully coordinated attacks against French military installations, public utilities, and communications facilities in 1954, a military parade attended by diplomatic delegations from a number of countries was held in Algiers on 1 November 1962. Established as the direct successor of the ALN, the National Popular Army (*Armée nationale populaire*, ANP) publicly displayed its weaponry for the first time. One of the highlights was Czechoslovak Praga V3S trucks towing guns which sparked various comments on the tribune for foreign diplomatic officials.

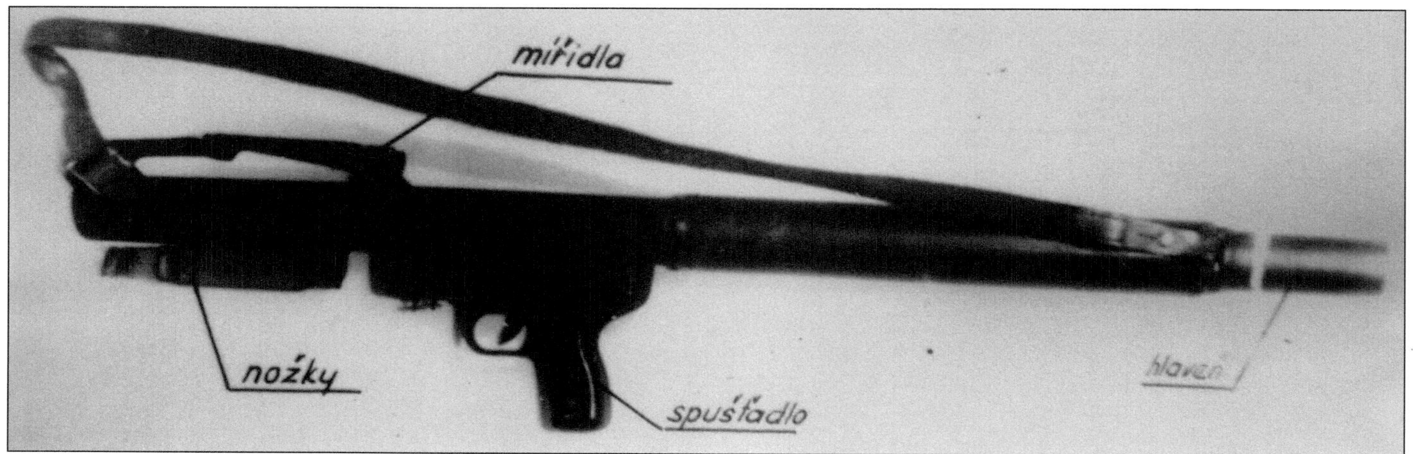

A launcher of the P-27 light anti-tank weapon, which, together with its associated ammunition, was manufactured in the first half of the 1950s at Závody Říjnové revoluce in Vsetín. (VÚA-VHA Praha)

The positive or negative attitude of the reaction depended upon whether the diplomat in question represented a Warsaw Pact or a NATO country. However, just one year passed before all Algerian V3S vehicles became immobile due to the shortage of spare parts.[21]

The fledgling regular armed forces of Algeria needed properly qualified technical experts for the maintenance and operation of the newly obtained weapon systems, delivered mostly from the Soviet Union. Against this background, Prague decided to play an active role in the training of new technical cadres for the ANP. Before independence, in November 1961, representatives of the GPRA approached an HTS official (who simultaneously served as the Czechoslovak business attaché) in Cairo with the request for the training of 25 to 30 students as aircraft mechanics for jet airplanes in Czechoslovakia. This demand was met with a positive reaction and thus the Politburo ÚV KSČ approved the undertaking in its resolution of 13 February 1962. The respective protocol between the Czechoslovak government and GPRA was signed on 27 March and 21 students from Cairo arrived in Czechoslovakia on 12 April. They were immediately sent to the Central Military Hospital (*Ústřední vojenská nemocnice*) in Prague for medical and bacteriological examination which took place between 13 and 16 April. The Algerians were issued with civilian clothes and transported to the Tactical-Technical Courses (*Takticko-technické kurzy*) section of the Aviation Training School (*Letecké učiliště*) at Přerov air base. They were joined by the final Algerian student one week later. All were aged between 16 and 20 years and most of them were separated from their families for three or more years either as students or former ALN combatants.[22]

The enterprise started on 24 April and received the Czechoslovak cover name Course 225. However, unlike the earlier training of the four artillery instructors, the training of aircraft technicians was plagued by their poor discipline and working morale. The situation escalated in the second part of June when two students, Khanfar Abdelbaki and Najib Bouzidi refused to obey Czechoslovak instructors and their commander Said. Bouzidi even threatened one of the instructors that he would 'smash his face in'. The Algerian representative in Prague, Mohamed Yalla, was informed about the problems in Přerov and he immediately requested the expulsion of both students and their sending back to Cairo. Moreover, he informed Czechoslovak representatives that Abdelbaki and Bouzidi would be sent to a punitive unit after they arrived in Algeria. Yalla personally visited Přerov on 3 July and spoke to the remaining students. Both wrongdoers were sent to Cairo during the same day.

The second problem was maintaining secrecy. Although the resolution of the Politburo ÚV KSČ ordered the utmost security measures in order to keep the origin of the cadets secret, it took only a couple of weeks before the true identity of the Algerians became an open secret. They were originally presented as Moroccans not only to other foreign students but to the instructor cadre in Přerov as well. Frequent visits by Yalla to Přerov caught the attention of one of the Malian students who, in May, showed the other cadets a Malian magazine with a photograph of Yalla in the company of Prague diplomatic representatives of Ghana, Guinea, and Mali together with Yalla's full name, nationality and official post. Algeria's independence from France came into being on 5 July 1962. Therefore, there was no further reason to classify the nationality of Algerian trainees. On 10 July, the Czechoslovak Minister of National Defence decided that the cover name Operation 130 was reserved for Algeria only. Subsequently, as a face-saving exercise, he ordered the commander of the training centre in Přerov to ceremonially announce this change on the base in order to strengthen the image of Czechoslovakia as a country that supported nations fighting for their freedom.[23]

After the initial six-week-long preparatory stage of the training, the Algerian students were divided into three groups according to their specialisation: airplane technicians – airframes and engines (13 students), electrical and special equipment technicians (four students), and communication equipment technicians (three students). The disciplinary problems re-emerged and in January 1963 Algerian representatives requested the dismissing of a further three students. The Czechoslovak instructors were not so harsh and decided to provide an opportunity for rectification by two students. Therefore, in the beginning, only Mohamed Nasri was fired. He was sent off home on 3 February 1963. However, Louardi Dass did not use the chance and his complete disinterest in the training resulted in his sacking and return flight on 21 April 1963. On the other hand, Mohamed Gasmi demonstrated marked improvement and successfully graduated from the course.

In the end, only 14 Algerians finished Course 225 in December 1963: eight airplane technicians, four electrical and special equipment technicians, and two communication equipment technicians. Four students were dismissed during the training. This was solely due to strict disciplinary demands of Algerian representatives including the commander of the Algerian Air Force, Said Ait-Messaoudene. The disciplinary problems of Course 225 were basically identical to other similar undertakings in which African or Middle Eastern soldiers were trained in Czechoslovakia. On 16 April 1963, following the request of Algerian officials, three students (Mohamed Said, Hadj Morsli, and Mustafa Krim) were sent to the preparatory course for their subsequent master's study at the Antonín Zápotocký Military Academy. While Mehrez Ben Laroussi completed only the theoretical part of the training because of his lung disease, Mahmoud Babahadi was more fortunate although he had pulmonary tuberculosis. He finished the training successfully under medical supervision and in January 1964 underwent surgery in University Hospital (*Fakultní Nemocnice*) Hradec Králové. His treatment continued there until 16 March 1964 after which he returned to Algeria. The remaining graduates from Course 225, including Mehrez Ben Laroussi, returned home on 23 December 1963. Algerian technicians received the theoretical and practical fundamentals in their specialisations in order to be able to perform their duties independently. Furthermore, the Czechoslovak officials informed their Algerian counterparts that the extent and the depth of the training enabled the promotion of the graduates into the officer ranks. Course 225 was provided free of charge for the Algerian Ministry of National Defence.[24]

TRAINING AT THE LF VAAZ

While Course 225 was in full swing, the Algerian Ministry of National Defence sent a letter with a wish for military training of further ANP members on 27 October 1962. Realising that the Algerian Air Force was in need of technical officers with master's degrees, the request for university education was submitted. The Politburo ÚV KSČ reacted affirmatively and approved this enterprise in its resolution from 20 November 1962. Thus, 12 young Algerians led by Idir Laribi arrived in Czechoslovakia on 7 February 1963. After the obligatory medical check-up in the Central Military Hospital in Prague, they were sent to the Tactical-Technical Courses at Přerov air base in order to attend the initial phase of their training. Its task was to prepare them for further studies at the Aviation Faculty of the Antonín Zápotocký Military Academy (*Letecká fakulta Vojenské akademie Antonína Zápotockého*, LF VAAZ) in Brno. Hence, most of the time was spent on teaching them the Czech language with the rest spent on mathematics, geometry, physics, descriptive geometry, technical drawing, and drill training. The training received Czechoslovak cover name Course 235.[25]

Following previous experience with Course 225, the commander of the Algerian Air Force insisted that Czechoslovak officials apply strict disciplinary rules upon the Algerian students. Therefore, the stay in Czechoslovakia ended prematurely for Mohamed Gheraia who was dismissed due to indiscipline and 'spreading of damaging opinions about socialism'. He returned to Algeria on 27 May 1963. In the meantime, three trainees from Course 225 joined their compatriots in their preparation for university studies. During June 1963, the training syllabus had to be changed in order to increase the number of Czech language teaching hours. The original allocation proved to be insufficient because the subsequent teaching at the VAAZ was conducted in the Czech language only. Although Czech was taught for less than seven months, the language skills that the students attained were considered very good. After the successful completion of the initial stage at Přerov, 14 Algerians became students of the LF VAAZ in Brno officially on 1 October 1963. They were divided into five specialisations: engineer of aircraft engines and airframes (five students), communication equipment engineer (three students), radar engineer (two students), aircraft electrical equipment and armament engineer (two students), and aircraft armament engineer (two students). Although their syllabus was shortened from the standard five years to just four, the scope of the education remained the same, except for the Russian language and studies of Marxism-Leninism which were removed.[26]

The previous positive assessment that the knowledge of the Czech language on the part of the Algerian students was adequate proved to be premature. At the beginning of their studies at the LF VAAZ it was apparent that the initial language course should have been more intensive and taken more time. Insufficient command of Czech caused many problems for the Algerians during the early stages of their studies in Brno. During 1965, the number of students on Course 235 was reduced to 12 because of the poor study results of two Algerians. Despite some complications, all remaining cadets managed to complete the studies successfully. The graduation ceremony took place on 29 July 1967 and all Algerians received the Czechoslovak *Inženýr* engineer's degree. Again, the education was provided free of charge. Four million CSK was provided for funding of both Courses 225 and 235. The Algerians returned home on 7, 8, 10, and 14 August. Quite surprisingly, four of them did that in their personal cars bought in Czechoslovakia and drove all the way back to Algeria.[27]

One of the buildings in the Brno–Černá Pole barracks that served as the garrison for the Foreign Faculty of the Antonín Zápotocký Military Academy. (Photo by Martin Smisek)

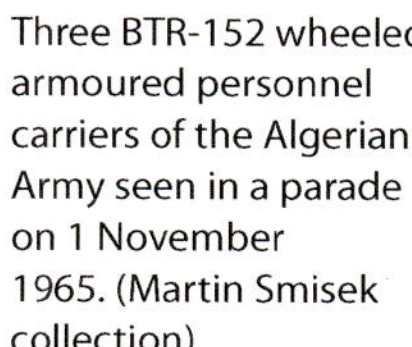

Three BTR-152 wheeled armoured personnel carriers of the Algerian Army seen in a parade on 1 November 1965. (Martin Smisek collection)

STAGNATION

Despite some early expectations, which were supported by the previous donation of arms and cost-free training of Algerian Air Force personnel in Czechoslovakia, commercial deliveries of armament to Algeria did not materialise. The main obstacle was the poor state of the Algerian economy with very minimal funds for the acquisition of weapons. However, this state of affairs did not hinder Moscow as they were ready to offer advanced weapons systems, such as MiG-21 fighters or SA-75 Dvina (NATO reporting name SA-2 Guideline) surface-to-air missile systems, under beneficial conditions in order to realise its political interests in Algiers. Hence, deliveries of Soviet weapons for the ANP during the 1960s took place free of charge or on favourable long-term credit with years of instalment postponements and great price reductions. Under such circumstances, the HTS decided to exert no initiative to arouse Algerian interest in the acquisition of the Czechoslovak armament.[28]

Therefore, only 50 vz. 53 tents and 1,000 blankets from the stocks of the Czechoslovak People's Army were apparently provided as a gift for the People's Democratic Republic of Algeria on the occasion of the Revolution Day commemoration on 1 November 1963. Until the end of the same year, spare parts for V3S trucks were probably delivered to Algeria free of charge as well.[29]

Any prospects of additional Czechoslovak military cooperation with Algiers were frustrated after the bloodless coup d'état which saw Algeria's first President, Ahmed Ben Bella, arrested and his closest supporters imprisoned on 19 June 1965. Minister of Defence Colonel Houari Boumédiène then rose to power as Chairman of the Revolutionary Council. He served in this position until 12 December 1976 and thereafter as the second President of Algeria until his death on 27 December 1978. However, these changes to the Algerian domestic political landscape led to the considerable freezing of political relations with Soviet Bloc countries, including Czechoslovakia.[30]

At the time of the coup, some 66,000 troops served with the ANP, which was reorganised in 1964 and as a consequence of the changes, the number of its service members was reduced. According to contemporary Czechoslovak intelligence information, the Algerian Ground Forces were composed of an infantry division deployed along the border with Morocco, an armoured division with 80 T-34/85 and T-54 tanks deployed at Laghouat, six armoured brigades armed with T-34/85 and T-54 tanks, and 75 infantry battalions. The Algerian Air Force was equipped with some 40 MiG-15 and MiG-17 fighters, six Ilyushin Il-28 bombers, and 16 Mil Mi-4 transport helicopters together with several training and liaison aircraft. On the other hand, the Algerian National Navy was still almost non-existent at that time. Training of Algerian military cadres abroad was in full swing. In 1964, some 500 officers returned from training in the Soviet Union (26 of them graduated from the Frunze Military Academy). A further 200 soldiers were undergoing military training in the Union of Soviet Socialist Republics in 1965. In this time, Algerian troops were also trained in the People's Republic of China (some 150 soldiers), Bulgaria (approximately 110 persons, some of them were civilians who underwent technical or another non-military schooling), the United Arab Republic (some 300 troops), and Yugoslavia (16 persons). A very small number of Algerian military personnel was trained in France as well. Simultaneously, foreign instructors operated on Algerian soil. The most numerous advisory teams came from the Soviet Union, the United Arab Republic, Cuba, and the People's Republic of China. Relatively large were the groups of instructors from France and West Germany that delivered communication equipment and vehicles (Magirus trucks and Volkswagen cars). Otherwise, the armament of the ANP was predominantly of Soviet origin.[31]

Algiers expressed its interest in the construction of a plant for the production of ammunition for infantry weapons in 1966. Although Prague was ready to realise such a project, no deal materialised.[32]

ATS-59 artillery tractors of the Algerian Army on parade in Algiers on 1 November 1967. (Martin Smisek collection)

Soviet-made T-54 medium tanks of the Algerian Army on parade in Algiers on 1 November 1967. (Martin Smisek collection)

LIMITED SUCCESS

During the early 1970s, the Czechoslovak communist leadership wanted to overcome the stagnation from the last years of the previous decade. The emphasis was laid on political relations between the KSČ and FLN together with the expansion of economic cooperation. Therefore, a delegation of the ÚV KSČ led by the secretary Vasil Biľak visited Algeria in May 1972 in order to break the ice. After the return to Czechoslovakia, the outcome of negotiations was described as the 'opening of a new chapter' in mutual relations. However, the early delight showed to be premature and the stagnation continued until the early 1980s.[33]

Table 7: Known Czechoslovak arms export to Algeria, 1970-1974[34]

Type	Number of examples	Year of delivery	Note
vz. 61, 7.65mm submachine gun	100	1970	from the stocks of the Czechoslovak People's Army
7.65mm round	1,000,000	1970	from the stocks of the Czechoslovak People's Army

Despite the unhelpful political background, the HTS was able to secure the first major contract for the supply of 12 Czechoslovak armoured support vehicles on the T-55 chassis, including spare parts, worth 2.5 million USD in 1976 (as listed in Table 8). The HTS officials assumed that the Algerian Ground Forces were in dire straits and needed this equipment badly because the Ministry of National Defence in Algiers accepted Czechoslovak payment conditions (company credit payable within one year) without much protest. Prague was more than satisfied – the attained prizes were lucrative and the Algerians paid their financial obligations properly. The Algerian Ministry of National Defence assessed the deal very positively as well – the delivered vehicles were considered to be high-quality and the activities of the Czechoslovak service team in Algeria were highly appreciated as well.[35]

Table 8: Deliveries of Czechoslovak armoured vehicles to Algeria, 1976–1977[36]

Type	Number of examples	Year of delivery	Note
JVBT-55 (JVBT-55KS), armoured crane vehicle	3	1976	newly manufactured
MT-55 (MT-55KS), armoured vehicle-launched bridge	4	1977	newly manufactured
VT-55 (VT-55KS), armoured recovery vehicle	5	1976	newly manufactured

The HTS exploited the opportunity to press home its business activity in Algiers. An additional 20 armoured support vehicles were offered in 1977. The Algerians expressed their interest but they conditioned the new contract upon more favourable payment conditions. During the negotiations by the HTS delegation with the top-ranking officials of Algerian Ministry of National Defence in 1978, the Algerians discussed the possibility of buying tanks, ammunition, L-39 Albatros training aircraft, and cooperation in the building of an ammunition plant. However, the Czechoslovak representatives were clearly aware that any deal was possible only with long-term credit under similar conditions that were provided by other communist countries. At that time, the Soviet Union still played the role of premier arms supplier. However, Bulgaria was active in Algeria too and, in 1977, granted credit to the value of 100 million USD for the acquisition of military materiel. The credits for arms deals were usually provided for 10 years with an interest rate of 2.5 %. Moreover, Prague's efforts to secure some major deal with Algiers were driven by not very optimistic prospects of Czechoslovak tank production after the year 1980. The largest Arab clients of the Czechoslovak arms industry, such as Syria, were showing the first signs of large-scale financial problems and it could potentially happen that the Czechoslovak's overgrown tank production capacities would remain only partially utilised, which could bring subsequent economic difficulties. Therefore, the communist leadership hoped that Algeria could serve at least partially as a replacement customer.[37]

Under such circumstances, on 14 September 1978, the government in Prague approved the granting of credit worth 50 million USD (728 million CSK) with an interest rate of 3 % that Algeria should use for the purchase of Czechoslovak weapons. However, the effort of the HTS proved to be fruitless again. The Algerians responded to the Czechoslovak offer only in 1980. They requested the delivery of T-55 tanks, the production of which had already halted at that time (no new orders were accepted) and replaced by the manufacture of much more modern T-72s. Thus, the credit remained untapped. Despite this setback, Prague did not become discouraged and Czechoslovak business representatives in Algeria continued in their endeavour and tried repeatedly to persuade Algerian military officials to buy Czechoslovak armament.[38]

A pair of BTR-50 armoured personnel carriers of the Algerian Army, in Algiers, in November 1969. (Martin Smisek collection)

TEMPORARY BREAKTHROUGH

In the meantime, in 1979 the Military Production Directorate of the Algerian Ministry of National Defence approached the HTS with a request for the construction of four military plants for the manufacturing of small arms, infantry ammunition, mines and grenades, and gunpowder and explosives. Czechoslovak Prime Minister Lubomír Štrougal approved further negotiations on this matter and thus, in October 1980, representatives of the HTS handed over to the Algerians corresponding technical studies and informal offers, including the estimated cost that could reach some 1.4 billion West German marks. Similar requests were sent by Algiers to Bulgaria and Yugoslavia as well. In the end, and identically to the previous instances, Prague was unsuccessful again.

Another important opportunity to offer Czechoslovak weapons came in late April 1984, when President of Algeria Chadli Bendjedid arrived in Prague and held two negotiations with his Czechoslovak counterpart Gustáv Husák. During the stay, Bendjedid and the accompanying delegation visited the Aero Vodochody aircraft manufacturing plant located in nearby Odolená Voda which served as a chance to present the most important products of the Czechoslovak arms industry, such as the L-39 Albatros jet trainer, L-410 light transport aircraft, BVP-1 infantry fighting vehicle, vz. 77 DANA self-propelled gun howitzer, vz. 70 multiple rocket launcher, Tatra 815 VT tractor truck, and Kladivo fire control system for the upgrading of T-55 tanks. Moreover, the Algerian delegation was informed about the technical specifications and operational capabilities of the KRTP-81 Ramona passive electronic intelligence system. Although Bendjedid expressed interest in the establishment of cooperation in the field of the military industry, including aircraft manufacturing, the immediate outcomes of his visit were completely negligible again.[39]

The specific negotiations related to the use of the credit worth 50 million USD offered in 1978 were restarted only in 1985. The Algerians were interested in spending the money on the acquisition of Czechoslovak training aircraft. Hence, a related credit agreement for the supply of Aero L-39 Albatros jet trainers and Zlin Z-142 piston trainer aircraft was signed in Algiers on 11 August 1986. These developments energised other officials from the Algerian Ministry of National Defence and three military delegations hurriedly visited Czechoslovakia during the first half of 1986. In intensive discussions with the HTS representatives, the Algerians forwarded a requirement for new credit that could be used for financing deliveries of T-72 tanks, support variants of the BVP-1 infantry fighting vehicle, and additional military materiel to the overall value of approximately 400 million USD. Granting of the credit was approved by the Czechoslovak government on 4 September 1986. This decision was confirmed later by the Presidium ÚV KSČ (*Předsednictvo ÚV KSČ*). The corresponding credit agreement to the value of 400 million USD was concluded on 12 October 1987. Simultaneously, three 'special' contracts worth 150 million USD covering the supply of Czechoslovak tanks (listed in Table 9) and BVP-1 infantry vehicles were signed as well. At the same time, two further contracts (financed through the credit agreement from August 1986) for the delivery of L-39 and Z-142 aircraft worth 42 million USD were awarded too.

In early October 1987, an Algerian delegation led by the Minister of Transportation General Rachid Benyelles visited Czechoslovakia in order to discuss the issue of the supply of L-410 aircraft, the modernisation of Algerian airports, the training of pilots and aircraft technicians, and most importantly the license production of Z-142 and Z-43 light sports and training aircraft in Algeria. The corresponding contract to the value of 15 to 20 million USD was duly signed. It was financed through the civilian credit provided by the Czechoslovak government. For the manufacturing of Czechoslovak aircraft in local conditions under the names Firnas-142 and Safir-43, the Algerian Ministry of National Defence established the company *Entreprise de Construction Aéronautique* located at Tafraoui air base, south of Oran.[40]

Table 9: Deliveries of tanks from Czechoslovakia to Algeria, 1986-1992[41]

Type	Number of examples	Year of delivery	Note
T-72M1, main battle tank	58	1987	newly manufactured
	48	1988	
T-72M1K, command tank	8	1988	newly manufactured

TRAINING AIRCRAFT FOR THE ALGERIAN AIR FORCE

In the mid-1980s, the Algerian Air Force found itself in the position of being equipped with the new generation of Soviet jet combat aircraft such as MiG-23 or MiG-25. However, its training units were still operating outdated Yak-18 and MiG-15UTI trainers. Moreover, a large part of new pilots underwent flying training abroad in the Soviet Union, Bulgaria, or Egypt (and later Czechoslovakia). In order to rectify this unsuitable situation, the leadership of the Algerian Air Force decided to establish a complex in-country training capability. As a user of combat airplanes from the Soviet Union, Algeria had basically no other proper choice than to select Czechoslovak L-39 Albatros jet training aircraft as a successor to its MiG-15UTI trainers. Simultaneously, Z-142s were ordered to fulfil the role of basic training aircraft. In the beginning, the first airplanes of this type were delivered directly from Czechoslovakia with the latter provided from domestic production.

After a series of negotiations, the Algerian Ministry of National Defence ordered the first 20 examples of L-39ZA training and light attack aircraft. The first batch of 10 airplanes was completed in 1987 and during the same year flown to Algeria. The remaining L-39ZAs were assembled and flown in the following year. Albatroses were introduced into the service of the 618th Advanced Training Squadron of the 8th Training Wing deployed at Tafraoui air base. The same wing operated Z-142 piston training aircraft as well. After the initial successful experience with the L-39ZAs, the Algerian Air Force decided to order an additional 12 airplanes of the same variant which were delivered in the summer of 1991.

A further seven L-39C Albatros airplanes were supplied five years later. These aircraft were originally built for the Soviet Air Force. However, the economically collapsing Soviet Union refused to take the ordered aircraft. Therefore, the unfinished Albatroses were offered to Algeria which accepted the Czech proposal. The aircraft were duly modified to have identical avionics standards as the already delivered L-39ZAs in service of the Algerian Air Force. As in the previous cases, the user of the airplanes became the 8th Training Wing.

Some of the Albatroses were later transferred at Mechria air base to the 2nd Training Wing and its subordinated unit, the 620th Advanced Training Squadron, which was responsible for tactical flying and instructor training. Its L-39ZAs were repeatedly operationally deployed to Ghriss airport in order to support ground forces fighting the insurgents in the western part of the country. The last 17 L-39ZA aircraft, originally built for Nigeria but not delivered due to the customer's financial difficulties, were delivered to Tafraoui during 2002 and 2004.[42]

Table 10: Overview of L-39 Albatros training aircraft delivered to Algeria, 1987–2004[43]

Year	Variant	Number of examples	Hand over, overflight
1987	L-39ZA.1	10	31 August 1987 – 28 September 1987
1988	L-39ZA.1	10	18 January 1988 – 15 February 1988
1991	L-39ZA.1	12	28 June 1991, 19 July 1991, 23 July 1991, 26 July 1991, 2 August 1991, 7 August 1991
1996	L-39C.1	7	21 July 1996, 27 July 1996
2002–2004	L-39ZA.4	17	2002–2004

DEBTS

Contrary to the dreams of Prague's communist leadership of the late 1980s, Algeria never became a solvent client ready to buy large numbers of Czechoslovak tanks like Syria and Libya did a decade earlier. This, in turn, was one of the reasons that during the first half of the 1990s led to large-scale problems in the Czechoslovak arms industry with its excessive armoured vehicle production capacities. As soon as the T-72M1 tanks were delivered to the Algerian Ground Forces, the country was rocked by the unexpected deadly disturbances of the 1988 October riots. The languishing economy due to low oil prices and widespread doubts about the ability of top-ranking Algerian military officers-cum-politicians to govern the country properly only increased the tensions in Algerian society. The riots of October 1988 resulted in political and economic changes which, however, ended up in the Algerian Civil War, a conflict between the government forces and various Islamic rebel groups which broke out in December 1991 and ravaged the country until February 2002.

Hence, despite all the invested efforts of various Czechoslovak officials to promote increased economic and military cooperation between the two states in the 1980s, the successor countries of communist Czechoslovakia, the Czech and Slovak Republic, could only count financial losses caused by Algerian inability to pay for the various civilian and military credits granted during the 1980s. Thus, as of 31 December 2004, the People's Democratic Republic of Algeria owed some 2.806 billion CZK (125.5 million USD) to the Czech Republic.[44]

The same aircraft seen looping and offering a better view of the pack with twin GSh-23 autocannon installed under the cockpit. (Aero Vodochody)

One of the L-39ZAs manufactured for Algeria seen during a pre-delivery test-flight in the Czech Republic. (Aero Vodochody)

2

MOROCCO (OPERATION 169; COUNTRY 663)

Communist Czechoslovakia recognised the independence of the Kingdom of Morocco on 20 June 1956. Several early Czechoslovak attempts to establish official diplomatic relations met no reaction from Rabat, though. Therefore, the Czechoslovak Ministry of Foreign Affairs (*Ministerstvo zahraničních věcí*) decided to set up at least business representation there. This office served not only for supporting Czechoslovak commercial interests in Morocco but as a home base for local intelligence activities of the StB (*Státní bezpečnost*, State Security) – the Czechoslovak communist secret police – operatives of which worked there under the disguise of business representatives.

During one such operation in May 1957, Czechoslovak intelligence officer František Vlček tried unsuccessfully to bribe and recruit an officer of Moroccan counter-intelligence. However, during the next meeting, Vlček was arrested and, after six weeks in prison, was expelled from the country. This scandal soured relations between Prague and Rabat for the subsequent period. Despite this setback, negotiations related to military deliveries were already in full swing. Since extensive deliveries of arms were destined for the large part for the FLN nationalist movement and its fighting against the French authorities in neighbouring French Algeria, details of these developments are mentioned in the chapter related to Algeria.[1]

PROBING DURING AND AFTER THE SAND WAR

The Algerian War ended in March 1962 with Algeria gaining its independence under the leadership of the FLN. However, peace in the region was very short-lived as Moroccan claims to portions of Algeria's Tindouf and Béchar provinces led to border conflict. The Sand War started on 25 September 1963 with fighting around the oasis towns of Tindouf and Figuig and the subsequent assault by Royal Moroccan Army units that captured two Algerian border posts at Hassi-Beida and Tindjoub. During a discussion with a Czechoslovak embassy official on 13 October 1963, the Moroccan Minister of Defence Mahjoubi Aherdane asked for urgent deliveries of 7.92mm rifles and mines to supply units fighting the Algerians and to replenish empty military warehouses. Unfortunately for the Moroccan minister, Czechoslovak stocks of surplus armament were depleted as well (First Secretary of the Communist Party of Czechoslovakia and President of Czechoslovakia Antonín Novotný opposed the deliveries of arms to Morocco at the time of the conflict anyway).[2]

Further Moroccan requests, issued through different West European arms trading companies and related to deliveries of four Klimov VK-1 jet engines for MiG-17 fighters and ammunition for Soviet weapons, met with a lukewarm reaction from the Main Technical Administration (*Hlavní technická správa*, HTS) of the

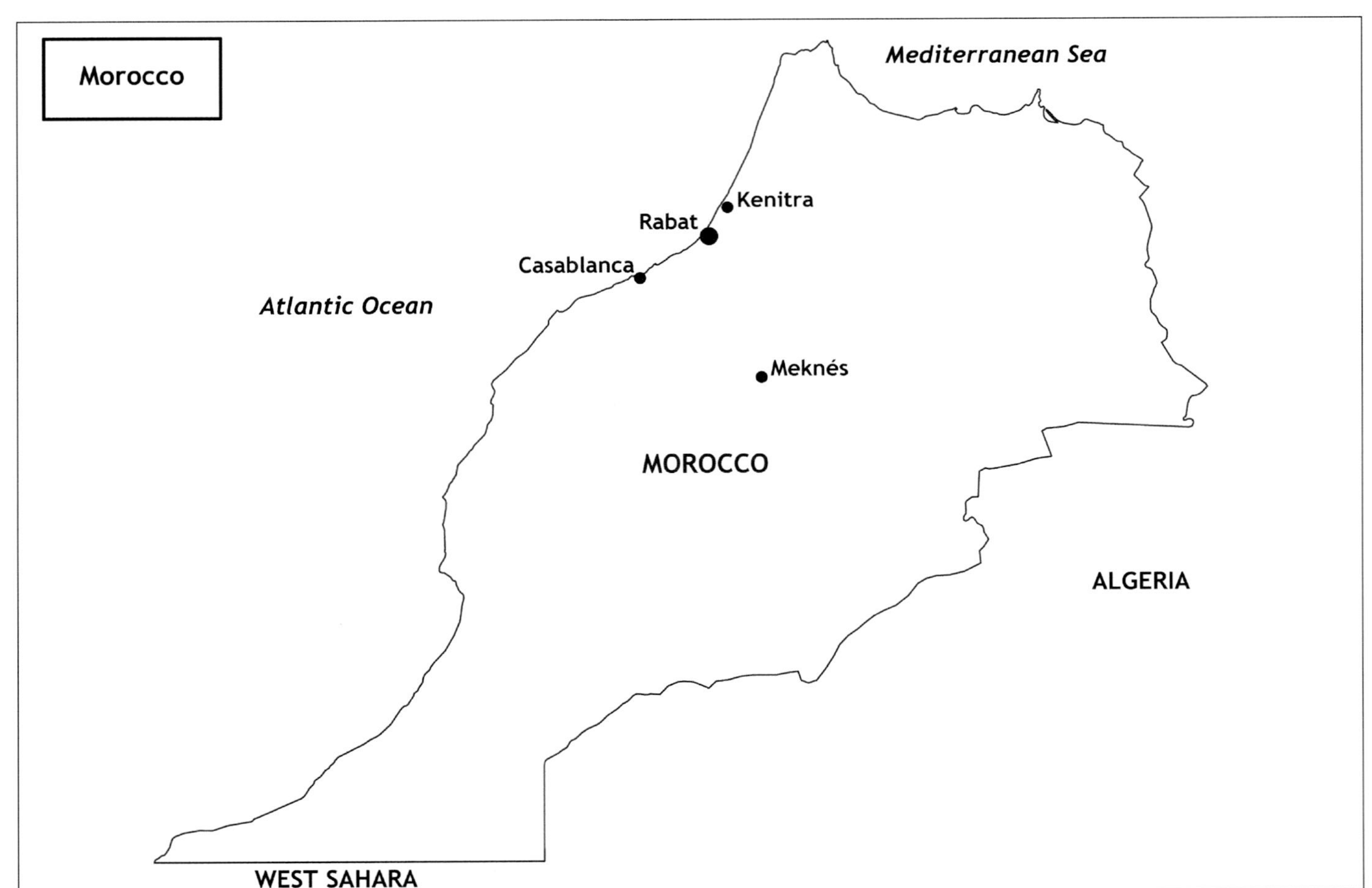

Map of places in Morocco mentioned in the text and related to the deliveries of arms and military facilities, as well as the activity of the Czechoslovak military advisors and specialists. (Map by b.b.h.illustrations)

Morocco received 12 MiG-17s directly from the USSR: four additional examples might have been delivered by 1962, but as of January of the following year relations with Moscow soured. The resulting lack of spare parts grounded the entire fleet by early 1963. Only a handful were operated during the Sand War with Algeria. (Albert Grandlini Collection)

Ministry of Foreign Trade (*Ministerstvo zahraničního obchodu*). This time, however, Algerian President Ahmed Ben Bella was informed about Moroccan intentions on 15 February 1964. He made an appeal to Czechoslovak officials that the deliveries would be limited to the lowest possible quantity and carried out for an extended period of time. Antonín Novotný approved the trade and Minister of National Defence Army General Bohumír Lomský agreed to provide four spare VK-1 engines (that would be re-exported from Poland) together with rifle, machine gun, mortar, and gun ammunition worth 64.9 million CSK. In the end, however, no deal materialised – the Moroccans started to discuss the matter of deliveries of engines and ammunition directly with Moscow.[3]

ARMOUR FOR THE ROYAL MOROCCAN ARMY

At that time, Morocco was the second most important business partner of Prague in the Arab world, right behind Egypt. Czechoslovakia imported phosphates, pyrolusite, oil cakes, exotic fruits, and fish in such amounts that the commercial balance ended with a trade deficit worth 42 million CSK in 1966. Considered by Prague as unacceptably high, the HTS was dispatched into action to sell a large number of arms and thus erase the negative balance of Czechoslovak trading with Morocco. The political situation was more than supportive of such activities. Moroccan King Hassan II wanted to increase the number of states delivering weapons for the Royal Armed Forces of Morocco in order to limit the influence of supplies from the United States of America. Moreover, the King's brother-in-law and new Minister of Defence Mohamed Cherkaoui supported the extension of cooperation with communist countries. During the second half of 1966, the Moroccan delegation held discussion with the representatives of the HTS related to deliveries of artillery and infantry ammunition together with spare parts for Soviet weapons supplied to Morocco during the years 1963 and 1964. However, only sometime later, Rabat managed to secure their deliveries directly from the Soviet Union. Therefore, Moroccan officials (Minister of Defence Mohamed Cherkaoui, Inspector General Driss Ben Omar El Alami, General Secretary of the Ministry of National Defence Colonel Driss Ben Aissa) requested the supply of 100 T-54A tanks with ammunition, 36 SD-100 self-propelled guns, at least 36 vz. 44 anti-aircraft guns including SON-9A radars

(i.e. six batteries), and general overhauls of MiG-17 fighters during the next round of negotiations with their Czechoslovak counterparts in early May 1967. At the end of the meeting, Minister of Defence Cherkaoui stated that the Moroccan side would appreciate the price reduction of tanks, provision of long-term credit, and rapid delivery of all requested weapons, ideally within a year.[4]

Since the Czechoslovak Air Force had no technical experts of their own that could carry out the overhauls of Moroccan MiG-17s, this request had to be turned down. Otherwise, the HTS was more than ready to comply with the demands of high-level Moroccan officials who had their own personal interest in a successful deal with Czechoslovakia. The Presidium (*Předsednictvo*) of the Central Committee of the Communist Party of Czechoslovakia (*Ústřední výbor Komunistické strany Československa*, ÚV KSČ) approved the deliveries of armament predominantly from the stocks of the Czechoslovak People's Army (*Československá lidová armáda*) to Morocco on credit up to the value of 150 million CSK on 13 June 1967. The resolution included an article that approved the payment of secret 'special commission to the amount of up to 2 % of the overall extent of deliveries' to respective Moroccan officials who arranged the deal under 'the optimal conditions for the Czechoslovak side'. The agreement worth 18 million USD (129 million CSK) between the Czechoslovak and Moroccan governments was signed in Rabat on 18 July 1967. Morocco was to pay one-third of the sum (6 million USD) during 1967. The remaining 12 million USD was to be paid in seven annual instalments from 1968 to 1974 with an interest rate of 4 %. Individual contracts on the delivery of the military hardware (Contract No. 31-7-20) and training of Moroccan crews and technicians were signed in Prague on 23 August 1967. The extent of deliveries is shown in Table 11. However, the Moroccans were not completely satisfied with the deal because Czechoslovakia delivered a lower number of tanks, with a limited amount of DShK anti-aircraft machine guns and without night vision devices for shooting (T-54A tanks were not equipped with sights for night-time operations). Therefore, in July, the Moroccan minister of defence presented a request for further 29 T-54A vehicles (including 10 examples of the command variant) together with DShK machine guns and night vision devices for all delivered tanks. Correspondingly, on 22 August 1967, the Presidium ÚV KSČ granted permission for further export of Czechoslovak military materiel to Morocco up to the overall value of 170 million CSK. Thus, the supply of an additional 29 tanks was approved (as listed in Table 12). The requirement for infrared night sights was turned down again on grounds of their shortages and mainly the need for relatively extensive adaptation of the turrets for their integration into the tanks. The agreement was signed by Moroccan Minister of Defence Echiguer in Prague on 19 September 1967. Thus, the scope of military deliveries from Czechoslovakia to Morocco reached an overall value of 22.4 million USD.[5]

The shipment of all materiel contracted under Contract No. 31-7-20 took place during three sailings of the Czechoslovak cargo ship *Brno* from the Yugoslav port of Rijeka between November 1967 and January 1968. An overall overview of Czechoslovak arms exports to Morocco during the years 1967 and 1968 is listed in Table 13.[6]

Table 11: Military deliveries to Morocco according to the Agreement from 18 July 1967 (Contract No. 31-7-20)[7]

Type	Number of examples	Unit price	Overall price	Note
T-54AR, medium tank	20	99,960 USD	1,999,200 USD	
T-54AR, medium tank	20	102,788 USD	2,055,760 USD	with DShK anti-aircraft machine gun
T-54ARK, command tank	10	103,787 USD	1,037,870 USD	with DShK anti-aircraft machine gun
SD-100, self-propelled gun	30	44,800 USD	1,344,000 USD	the Czechoslovak licensed Soviet SU-100, after general overhaul
OT-62, armoured personnel carrier	30	55,000 USD	1,650,000 USD	including two DTP-62 armoured repair vehicles
OT-64, armoured personnel carrier	70	53,000 USD	3,710,000 USD	including four DTP-64 armoured repair vehicles
V-54, engine	5	11,859 USD	59,295 USD	spare engine for T-54AR/T-54ARK
V-2, engine	5	8,568 USD	42,840 USD	spare engine for SD-100
PV-6, engine	3	10,480 USD	31,440 USD	spare engine for OT-62
T-928-14, engine	7	3,500 USD	24,500 USD	spare engine for OT-64
Tatra 141, tractor truck	28	14,583 USD	408,324 USD	
P-63, low-loading trailer	20	20,628 USD	412,560 USD	
TPDA-R, mobile tank workshop	3	14,960 USD	44,880 USD	on Praga V3S chassis
mobile workshop for repairs of accumulators	2	9,640 USD	19,280 USD	on Praga V3S chassis, could be used as a mobile station for recharging of accumulators
JT-34, crane tank	4	56,500 USD	226,000 USD	
spare parts for T-54AR for two years of service	-	-	600,000 USD	
spare parts for SD-100 for two years of service	-	-	150,000 USD	
spare parts for OT-62 for two years of service	-	-	250,000 USD	
spare parts for OT-64 for two years of service	-	-	400,000 USD	
spare parts for special vehicles for two years of service	-	-	40,000 USD	
spare parts for Tatra 141 and P-63 for two years of service	-	-	100,000 USD	
T-54 lecture room	1	238,790 USD	238,790 USD	
SD-100 lecture room	1	35,910 USD	35,910 USD	
OT-62 lecture room	1	73,270 USD	73,270 USD	
OT-64 lecture room	1	58,295 USD	58,295 USD	
ÚNOR, mobile loading ramp	2	42,250 USD	84,500 USD	
100-JOF-ShK 44, K 53, TK, 100mm high explosive round	16,700	81.20 USD	1,356,040 USD	
100-JPrSv-TK, 100mm high explosive anti-tank round	7,300	126 USD	919,800 USD	
12,7-PZ, 12.7mm armour-piercing incendiary round	37,500	510 USD (for 1,000 rounds)	19,125 USD	
12,7-PZSv, 12.7mm armour-piercing incendiary round with tracer	7,500	580 USD (for 1,000 rounds)	4,350 USD	
vz. 59, 7.62mm round	675,000	69 USD (for 1,000 rounds)	46,575 USD	
vz. 59 Sv, 7.62mm round with tracer	75,000	75 USD (for 1,000 rounds)	5,625 USD	
different material	-	-	551,771 USD	10 MOV mine ploughs, 10 VO trailers with mine-clearing line charge, four DG 321 welding sets, two Praga V3S – A0 mobile workshops, five R-112 and 10 R-113 reserve radio stations, etc.

Table 12: Additional order of tanks and ammunition in 1967[8]

Type	Number of examples	Note
T-54AR, medium tank	24	six tanks with DShK anti-aircraft machine gun
T-54ARK, command tank	5	
100-JOF-ShK 44, K 53, TK, 100mm high explosive round	5,800	Contract No. 21-7-82
100-JPrSv-TK, 100mm high explosive anti-tank round	2,900	Contract No. 21-7-82
12,7-PZ, 12.7mm armour-piercing incendiary round	22,500	Contract No. 21-7-82
12,7-PZSv, 12.7mm armour-piercing incendiary round with tracer	4,500	Contract No. 21-7-82
vz. 59, 7.62mm round	400,000	Contract No. 21-7-82
vz. 59 Sv, 7.62mm round with tracer	50,000	Contract No. 21-7-82

Table 13: Czechoslovak arms export to Morocco, 1967-1968[9]

Type	Number of examples	Year of delivery	Note
Sa 23 and Sa 25, 9mm submachine gun	500	1967	
vz. 61, 7.65mm submachine gun	2	1967	a gift for Moroccan top military officials (including King Hassan II)
vz. 52, 7.62mm rifle	4,000	1967	
vz. 59 N, 7.62mm machine gun	300	1967	a version of vz. 59 general purpose machine gun for the NATO round (7.62x51mm)
7.65mm round	200	1967	
vz. 48, 9mm round	1,000,000	1967	
vz. 52, 7.62mm round	1,000,000	1967	
vz. 59, 7.62mm round	750,000	1967	
	450,000	1968	
T-54AR, medium tank	64	1967	26 tanks delivered with DShK anti-aircraft machine gun
T-54ARK, command tank	15	1967	10 tanks delivered with DShK anti-aircraft machine gun
SD-100, self-propelled gun	30	1967	
JT-34, crane tank	4	1967	
	3	1968	
100-JOF-ShK 44, K 53, TK, 100mm high explosive round	16,700	1967	
	5,800	1968	
100-JPrSv-TK, 100mm high explosive anti-tank round	7,300	1967	
	2,090	1968	
12,7-PZ and 12,7-PZSv, 12.7mm armour-piercing incendiary round	44,500	1967	ammunition for DShK machine gun
	27,000	1968	
OT-62, armoured personnel carrier	30	1967	including two DTP-62 armoured repair vehicles
OT-64, armoured personnel carrier	70	1967	including four DTP-64 armoured repair vehicles
TPDA-R, mobile tank workshop	3	1967	
RM-31S, radio station	5	1967	
PNV-57, night vision goggles for drivers	70	1968	from Czechoslovak license production, for OT-64 armoured personnel carriers
spare parts for infantry weapons	672,200 CSK	1967	
spare parts for T-54AR tanks	4,453,000 CSK	1967	
spare parts for armoured vehicles	840,000 CSK	1968	
spare parts for communication equipment	228,100 CSK	1967	

Note: Deliveries of Tatra 141 trucks, P-63 low-loading trailers, and some other vehicles including related spare parts and accessories were handled through Motokov foreign trading company as civilian material.

TRAINING OF MOROCCAN SOLDIERS

The short-term, but intensive training of 30 future Moroccan technical instructors (listed in Table 14) led by 1st Lieutenant Achir Moulay Abdellaziz was ordered and paid for under Contract No. 52717. It started under the cover name Course 199A at the Foreign Faculty of the Antonín Zápotocký Military Academy (*Zahraniční fakulta Vojenské akademie Antonína Zápotockého*, ZF VAAZ) in Brno on 15 September 1967. The undertaking was complicated by the low technical expertise of the Moroccan students together with their insufficient practical experience and inadequate technical education. However, these complications were overcome thanks to the hard work and intensive study by the Moroccan soldiers that was supported by additional consultations provided by Czechoslovak teachers. Therefore, the course was concluded successfully with good results and the Moroccan soldiers returned back home after six weeks of their stay in Czechoslovakia.[10]

Table 14: Course 199A, training of Moroccan instructors at the ZF VAAZ[11]

Specialisation	Number of instructors
technical instructor for T-54AR	6
weapon instructor for T-54AR	6
instructor for OT-62	4
instructor for OT-64	6
technical instructor for SD-100	4
weapon instructor for SD-100	4

While the Moroccan trainees were finishing their education at Brno, a team of 11 Czechoslovak military advisors and five interpreters was dispatched directly to Morocco in order to provide training for local troops. The teaching activity of the Czechoslovak instructors was awarded as Contract No. 52716. Although they arrived in Morocco on 26 October 1967, no one paid attention to their presence. Respective Moroccan officials were absolutely not ready for their arrival and, moreover, they were overwhelmed by preparations for a military parade at Kenitra. On 1 November, the

Czechoslovak advisory team moved to the Armoured Training Centre (*Centre d'Instruction des Blindés*) at Meknés. The unit, led by Major Mohammed Madkour, was established just two years earlier in a former military warehouse. Proper training equipment was almost non-existent, except for several deteriorated teaching aids for Soviet T-54 tanks, French AMX-13 light tanks, and EBR armoured cars. The only vehicles available for driver training were just two T-54 chassis. At the time of Czechoslovak arrival, the buildings of former warehouses were provisionally prepared for the installation of Czechoslovak lecture rooms ordered under Contract No. 31-7-20. The working conditions at Meknés were very rudimentary, with offices without typewriters, an adequate number of desks, and any reasonable means of heating.

Czechoslovak advisors went immediately into work and organised a five-month-long training course for tank platoon commanders on T-54AR tanks. The training was divided into two stages. The first phase, composed of technical instruction, started on 20 November 1967 and was taught by Czechoslovak advisors. The follow-on tactical portion continued from February 1968 and was led by Moroccan officers only. The first group of trainees comprised 17 fresh graduates of Meknés Royal Military Academy with the rank of 2nd Lieutenant. The course for T-54AR and OT-62 crews from a tank brigade deployed at Rabat was launched on 11 December 1967. For this purpose, four T-54AR tanks and four OT-62 armoured personnel carriers, recently delivered from Czechoslovakia, were transferred to the Armoured Training Centre at Meknés. Since most Moroccan crewmembers did not understand the French language, the training was led by Moroccan instructors, graduates of Course 199A, under the guidance of Czechoslovak advisors.

However, to the dissatisfaction of the Czechoslovak instructors, Royal Moroccan Army officials preferred quantitative aspects of training – to prepare the maximum number of crews in the given time as possible, without regard to the quality of skills attained in the training courses. Activities of the Czechoslovak advisory team in Morocco ended on 30 April 1968.[12]

A Czechoslovak-manufactured T-54AR of the Moroccan army seen crossing the border from Morocco to the former Spanish Sahara (Western Sahara) in mid-December 1975. (Albert Grandolini collection)

A Czechoslovak-manufactured OT-62 armoured personnel carrier knocked out during the insurgent attack on the base of the 3rd Mechanised Regiment of the Moroccan Army outside Lebouirat, Western Sahara, in August 1979. (Albert Grandolini collection)

Also knocked out during the same attack on the base of the 3rd Mechanised Regiment of the Moroccan Army was this Czechoslovak-manufactured T-54AR. According to the Moroccans, all the vehicles knocked out during the same attack – including 37 T-54s and 13 OT-62s – had been non-operational for months. (Albert Grandolini collection)

COURSES AT THE ZF VAAZ

To secure proper maintenance and repairs of Czechoslovak armour under local conditions, the further training of 29 Moroccan soldiers was conducted in two courses at the ZF VAAZ, each lasting six months, beginning 1 November 1967 (as listed in Table 15).

Table 15: Courses 263 and 266, training of Moroccan technical personnel at the ZF VAAZ[13]

Training course	Specialisation	Number of students
Course 263	technician of T-54 and SD-100	8
	tank armament technician	5
Course 266	ammunition technician	3
	communication equipment technician	5
	mechanised unit technician	8

However, the period of the most extensive training of Moroccan soldiers in Czechoslovakia was yet to start. On 18 October 1968, representatives of the Czechoslovak HTS and Moroccan Ministry of National Defence signed Supplement No. 2 and No. 3 of Contract No. 52717 which paved the way for the training of up to 122 Moroccan military specialists in 16 different technical courses related to armoured vehicles delivered recently from Czechoslovakia, together with artillery armament (D-44 field guns, KS-19 anti-aircraft guns, SON-9A fire control radars, and PUAZO 6-19 fire control directors) supplied by Moscow in 1962. Because of the lack of qualified crews and maintenance personnel, these guns and related equipment from the Soviet Union were basically not used, only with the exception of public presentation at military parades.

All courses for the Moroccan military technical personnel were organised at the ZF VAAZ in Brno. In some cases, the practical training took place at different military repair plants of the Czechoslovak Federal Ministry of National Defence (*Federální ministerstvo národní obrany*).[14] Contrary to the terms of the contract, the Royal Moroccan Army sent to Czechoslovakia many soldiers who did not comply with requirements concerning the level of attained education and craftsmanship. Thus, the training was generally complicated by the limited or almost non-existent theoretical knowledge of Moroccan students. This, in turn, placed greater strain on Czechoslovak teachers. However, the trainees usually worked hard to reduce this deficiency and were eager to learn as much as possible. The first courses started in the middle of January 1969 and the last ones ended in early February 1970. The scope of the training is detailed in Table 16.[15]

The ZF VAAZ was ready to provide an academic education for Moroccan service members as well. However, such an undertaking took place apparently only once. Code-named Course 312, one Moroccan citizen (probably Major Amezil from the military repair plant at Casablanca) was to study the master's degree programme in Brno during June 1969 and April 1974.[16]

STAGNATION

Representatives of the HTS and Moroccan Ministry of National Defence signed Contract No. 4390004 worth 197,138 USD in Rabat on 31 December 1969. The deal aimed to establish the capability to repair T-54AR tanks, SD-100 self-propelled guns, OT-62 and OT-64 armoured personnel carriers, and Tatra 141 trucks at the military repair plant at Casablanca. Repair Plant 026 (*Opravárenský závod 026*) at Šternberk became the Czechoslovak main contractor that was responsible for the delivery of metalworking machines, accessories, assembly carts and jigs, special tools, and technical documentation containing more than 2,400 drawings and 3,200 pages with the description of respective repair processes.

Originally in 1968, Repair Plant 026, INPRO Praha, and the Military Design Institute (*Vojenský projektový ústav*) prepared an

Table 16: Courses 284 to 299, training of Moroccan military personnel at the ZF VAAZ[17]

Training course	Specialisation	Number students	Duration of the training
Course 284	technician of T-54AR, SD-100, OT-62, and OT-64	7	15 September 1969 – 11 September 1970
Course 285	mechanic of T-54AR and SD-100	13	6 February 1969 – 3 September 1969
Course 286	mechanic of T-54AR	9	6 February 1969 – 11 June 1969
Course 287	technician of T-54AR	7	2 April 1969 – 10 September 1969
Course 288	mechanic of STP-1 gun stabiliser (T-54AR)	5	2 April 1969 – 23 July 1969
Course 289	ammunition technician – bomb disposal expert	6	15 January 1969 – 2 July 1969
Course 290	mechanic of OT-62 and OT-64	17 (2 dismissed because of poor discipline)	2 April 1969 – 23 January 1970
Course 291	mechanic of radio stations (R-120, R-112, R-113, RM-31Sa)	14	26 March 1969 – 29 October 1969
Course 292	technician of T-54 armament	8	15 January 1969 – 30 July 1969 (follow-up study of 4 students until 9 February 1970)
Course 293	specialist in injection pumps of V-54, V-2, PV-6, and T-928-14 engines	7	26 March 1969 – 25 June 1969
Course 294	artillery technician of D-44 and KS-19	2	6 February 1969 – 5 February 1970
Course 295	artillery technician of D-44	9	6 February 1969 – 28 November 1969
Course 296	artillery technician of KS-19	5	6 February 1969 – 28 November 1969
Course 297	technician of SON-9A	5	6 February 1969 – 5 February 1970
Course 298	technician of PUAZO 6-19	5	6 February 1969 – 5 February 1970
Course 299	technician of optical devices for T-54AR, SD-100, OT-62, OT-64, D-44, and KS-19	2	15 January 1969 – 2 July 1969

offer for the complete construction of a brand new repair facility for vehicles supplied from Czechoslovakia. However, the Moroccan authorities turned this project down and opted only for the delivery of required repair equipment that would be installed in an already existing repair plant at Casablanca. The first stage of deliveries was underway in December 1970. It was followed by supplies of the second phase that was to take place during July and August 1971. Delivered equipment was installed under the guidance of specialists from Repair Plant 026 who then functioned as supervisors during the start-up of the facility. According to the plan, the military repair plant at Casablanca, modified for repairs of Czechoslovak vehicles, was to be handed over to Moroccan authorities in January 1972.[18]

However, this was already a swan song in the Czechoslovak-Moroccan military cooperation. Beginning in the early 1970s, political relations between Prague and Rabat stagnated. At that time, Morocco was considered by Czechoslovak communists as a pro-Western country controlled by the King's dictatorship. Therefore, under these circumstances, Prague had a lukewarm attitude towards the securing of additional large-scale deliveries of arms or training

for Moroccan troops. This stance was further strengthened after 1975 when the Western Sahara War broke out between Morocco and POLISARIO (*Popular de Liberación de Saguía el-Hamra y Río de Oro*) national liberation movement. Czechoslovak communists sided with Sahrawi rebels during that armed struggle. However, while Moroccan armour delivered from Czechoslovakia was fighting the insurgents, Prague was providing only verbal support to the representatives of POLISARIO. Despite their numerous requests for material help, the Czechoslovak officials were mostly ready to provide just words of moral backing.[19]

Table 17: Known Czechoslovak arms export to Morocco, 1970-1974[20]

Type	Number of examples	Year of delivery	Note
vz. 61, 7.65mm submachine gun	6	1972	from the stocks of the Czechoslovak People's Army
	1	1973	from the stocks of the Czechoslovak People's Army

A Czechoslovak-made JT-34 armoured engineering recovery vehicle seen after being recaptured by the Moroccans from the ELPS insurgents (military wing of the POLISARIO Front), in the Mabhas-Farcia area of the Western Sahara, in October 1987. (Albert Grandolini collection)

3

LIBYA (COUNTRY 658, OPERATION 737, OPERATION LITOMYŠL), PART A – UP TO 1979

Libya achieved independence on 24 December 1951, as the United Kingdom of Libya. The newly emerged constitutional monarchy ruled by King Idris initially attained only a little attention from the communists in Prague. Czechoslovakia's interest in establishing diplomatic relations with Libya began to grow in the mid-1950s after extensive contracts for the supply of Czechoslovak weapons were concluded with neighbouring Egypt. In November 1956, the Czechoslovak embassy in Cairo proposed to Libyan representatives the establishing of diplomatic relations between both countries.

However, this proposition met almost no reaction. Thus, diplomatic relations were not established until 1960 with the opening of the Czechoslovak embassy in Tripoli. The Libyan royal regime did not show much interest in Czechoslovakia, so mutual relations were limited to undertakings of a formal nature. Besides, unlike other countries in the Middle East or Sub-Saharan Africa, there were no left-wing forces with which the Czechoslovak communist regime could establish contacts.[1]

Nevertheless, the Main Technical Administration (*Hlavní technická správa*, HTS) of the Ministry of Foreign Trade (*Ministerstvo zahraničního obchodu*) managed to create contacts with Libyan private trading companies under the disguise of foreign trade company OMNIPOL. However, only minor arms contracts were signed. For example, in 1967, 4,575 rounds of 7.65mm ammunition from the stocks of the Czechoslovak People's Army were delivered to the Headquarters Security Forces at Bayda.[2]

However, this situation was to change in a very short time, and during the late 1970s and early 1980s, Libya became the most important and solvent client of Czechoslovak military hardware in the Middle East.

King Idris of Libya (left, seated), the ruler of the United Kingdom of Libya from 1951 until 1969. (Albert Grandolini collection)

1 SEPTEMBER REVOLUTION AND ITS CONSEQUENCES

The situation with regard to the supply of military hardware to Libya changed sharply in 1969. A decade earlier, significant oil reserves were discovered on Libyan territory. The income from petroleum sales enabled the Kingdom of Libya to transition rapidly from one of the world's poorest countries to a wealthy state. Since the nation's wealth was concentrated in the hands of King Idris, over time discontent in different parts of Libyan society began to mount. These developments culminated on 1 September 1969 when a group of rebel military officers, led by Captain Muammar Gaddafi, launched a successful coup d'état against the Libyan ruler. The country was proclaimed the Libyan Arab Republic (the official name was changed to the Socialist People's Libyan Arab Jamahiriya in 1977) and was run by the Revolutionary Command Council (RCC) that constituted the Libyan government after the coup. Captain Gaddafi was subsequently promoted to the rank of colonel and was recognised as both chairman of the RCC as well as the commander-in-chief of the armed forces, becoming the *de facto* head of state.

The Czechoslovak embassy in Tripoli was quite disoriented by Gaddafi's swift putsch and thus Prague recognised the new regime on 7 September 1969. Although the new Libyan government categorically rejected communism, Gaddafi attracted the attention of the Soviet Bloc countries due to his 'anti-imperialist and anti-colonialist approach'. At the same time, the socialist countries expected the nationalisation of facilities belonging to foreign oil companies that operated their businesses in Libya. In addition, Gaddafi's impression in the communist states benefited from the liquidation of American and British bases in the country in 1970.

Simultaneously, Libya began considering purchasing weapons from Soviet Bloc countries based on direct deals without Egyptian mediation. Therefore, Gaddafi asked Egypt to provide appropriate contacts for the acquisition of military hardware in Eastern Europe, but not in the Soviet Union, on which he did not want to be dependent. These developments paved the way for the active involvement of the HTS. The first talks between HTS officials (acting officially in the name of foreign trade company OMNIPOL) and

A British-made Saladin armoured car of the Royal Libyan Army seen during a military parade in al-Bayda in 1958. (Martin Smisek collection)

ALGERIA

The BVP-1 was the Czechoslovak version of the 13,000kg, Soviet-designed BMP-1 infantry fighting vehicle, manufactured under license from 1971. It was manufactured by ZŤS Dubnica nad Váhom (for the Soviet Army) and PPS Detva (for Czechoslovakia and other export customers outside the Soviet Union). Its principal armament was the vz. 71, the Czechoslovak variant of the original 2A28 Grom 73mm gun. This was coupled with a Soviet-made PKT 7.62mm machine gun. Because of its higher manufacturing quality, it was much coveted by customers abroad, despite its higher price. (Artwork by David Bocquelet)

Under the credit agreement concluded in October 1987, Algeria was to receive, between 1988 and 1990, among other equipment, 70 BVP-1 infantry fighting vehicles, 40 AMB-1 ambulance vehicles, and 45 VPV armoured recovery vehicles. As shown by its raised superstructure and roof, and the insignia of red crescent on a white circle, the vehicle illustrated here is an AMB-1 manufactured for Algeria and delivered in the late 1980s. It could take four stretcher patients inside, and was also equipped with an additional infrared searchlight (not shown here). (Artwork by David Bocquelet)

Under the contract from 1987, Algeria acquired a total of 106 Czechoslovak-manufactured T-72M1 main battle tanks and 8 T-72M1K command tanks. Illustrated here is one of the former, in the typical camouflage pattern of the Algerian People's National Army, which includes dark brown and dark green. (Artwork by David Bocquelet)

A reconstruction of one of the 57 Firnas-142 – Zlin Z-142Cs – delivered starting in 1987 in the form of knock-down kits and assembled by the *l'Entreprise de Construction Aéronautique de Tafraoui*. Initially painted in ivory (similar to the Czechoslovak colour 6003 *slonová kost* or BS381C/388 beige) and dark brown (similar to the BS381C/450) on top surfaces and sides, and wearing civilian registrations, as shown here, the aircraft were operated by the 650th and the 658th Elementary Training Flights of the 65th Training Squadron, and the 670th and 678th Elementary Training Flights of the 67th Training Squadron, all based at Oran AB. In the 1990s, these were reorganised as the 658th and 678th Basic Training Squadrons of the 8th Training Wing, and moved to Tafraoui AB. (Artwork by Tom Cooper)

Since undergoing overhauls at the works in Tafraoui, in the 2000s, the Algerian Air Force's Zlin Z-142s have received a slightly darker livery, including the colour similar to the Czechoslovak 6050 *krémová světlá* (light cream) and 6700 *okr světlý* (light ochre) on top surfaces and sides, and 4265 *modř pastelová* (light blue) on undersides. Moreover, spinners, wing-, fin-, and tailfin tips were painted in day-glo orange. All have retained their civilian registrations but often wear squadron crests on the fin. The type remains the principal elementary and basic trainer of the Algerian Air Force. (Artwork by Tom Cooper)

Between 1987 and 1991, Algeria acquired a total of 32 L-39ZAs. For most of the first 15 years of their operational service, they were assigned to the 618th Squadron at Tafraoui AB, and the 620th Squadron 'Tigers' at Mecheria, and employed for basic jet training, weapons training, and preparing future pilots for MiGs and Sukhois of the Algerian air force. Additionally, through the 1990s and early 2000s, the type flew numerous combat sorties against Islamist insurgents, usually armed with UB-16-57 pods for S-5K unguided 57mm rockets, as shown here. (Artwork by Tom Cooper)

Reinforced through seven additional L-39C.1s originally manufactured for the Soviet Air Force – and delivered in 1997 – in the late 2000s, all of the Algerian Albatroses were grouped into the 618th and the 620th Advanced Training Squadrons, both assigned to the Air Force Academy at Tafraoui. Over the following years, all the surviving airframes underwent overhaul with the help of Czech technicians. All the L-39ZAs of what was now the 620th Squadron 'Tigers' – including serial numbers NL-15, NL-49, NL-55, NL-57, NL-68 and NL-88 – received different variants of this highly attractive 'tiger' pattern. (Artwork by Tom Cooper)

The last 17 Albatroses acquired by Algeria were all completed to the L-39ZA.4 standard: they were originally manufactured for a Nigerian order, which was never delivered due to funding shortfalls. They are easily recognisable by their noses, wing-tip drop tanks and fins painted in day-glo orange, slightly different colours used in their camouflage pattern (including 6003 ivory and dark brown), and a prominent pod for the twin-barrel GSh-23 gun under the forward cockpit. Their known serials are NL-12, NL-14, NL-19, NL-26, NL-29, NL-28, NL-43, NL-45, NL-56, NL-59, NL-67, NL-72, NL-75, and NL-82 – of which only four (NL-34, -56, -59, and 72) were seen wearing the unit insignia of the fin. (Artwork by Tom Cooper)

MOROCCO

Morocco was one of the first export customers for the OT-62 TOPAS – an upgraded variant of the BTR-50PA armoured personnel carrier manufactured in Czechoslovakia under license. The basic OT-62 variant delivered to Morocco was equipped with a small rotating turret mounting the vz. 59T 7.62mm general purpose machine gun. These became the principal mounts of the 1° and 3°GEB – armoured groups the size of a regiment, each including 30 APCs and 60 main battle tanks, and created in the late 1960s for the purpose of being deployed to Syria in the event of another war with Israel. The last were withdrawn from service in 1982. (Artwork by David Bocquelet)

Starting in 1967, Morocco acquired a total of 70 Czechoslovak-built OT-64 armoured personnel carriers. Like the OT-62s, they were distributed evenly between the 1°, 2° and 3° GEB. Notably, instead of the turret originally designed for the BRDM-2 armoured scout car, they had the same small turret for the vz. 59T 7.62mm general purpose machine gun as used on the OT-62 TOPAS. While none are known to have been deployed to Syria in 1973, they saw intensive deployment during the war in the Western Sahara of 1975–1991, where the Moroccans appreciated their higher speed and better all-terrain mobility than that of tracked vehicles. The pictured vehicle operated from the military camp at Bou Craa in Western Sahara in January 1976. (Artwork by David Bocquelet)

The JT-34 consisted of the chassis and hull of the T-34 tank, fitted with a heavy superstructure with a crane instead of the usual gun turret. The crane could lift loads up to 10,000kg in field conditions and was designed for removing and mounting complete turrets, guns, and engines. Morocco acquired only seven, in 1967 and 1968, but they saw heavy service in-country and during the deployment of the 3°GEB to Syria in 1973. They were later employed in the Western Sahara, where at least one was captured by the local insurgents, and then recovered by the Royal Moroccan Army. (Artwork by David Bocquelet)

A Czechoslovak-made T-54AR of the 3° GEB, Royal Moroccan Army, as seen crossing the border from Morocco to the Spanish Sahara in mid-December 1975. Initially left green overall – and regularly wearing a wide white stripe applied atop of their turret for easier identification from the air, at least during the deployment to Syria in 1973 – by 1975 Moroccan T-54ARs were all painted in yellow sand overall, and wore large, four-digit turret numbers (3922 in this case). As well as deployment to Syria during the October 1973 Arab-Israeli War, they saw intensive operations in the Western Sahara during the late 1970s and throughout the 1980s, when a number were captured by local insurgents and turned against their original users. (Artwork by David Bocquelet)

Captain Gaddafi seen during a public appearance immediately after the revolution of 1969. (Martin Smisek collection)

Libyan representatives took place as early as 1970 and were allegedly mediated by the Egyptian Minister of the Interior.[3]

Thus, the first major contract was signed on 9 December 1970. Within this frame, Czechoslovakia delivered 100 OT-62 TOPAS armoured personnel carriers to Libya with Soviet approval.

Additional contracts followed shortly thereafter so that between 1970 and 1973, 100 OT-62s, 145 T-55 tanks in various versions, ammunition for infantry weapons, spare parts for the supplied vehicles, and technical equipment for the armoured vehicles repair plant were delivered to Libya (for more details see Table 18). The value of these deliveries reached almost 80 million DM (approximately 650 million CSK).[4]

TURNING POINT

The Libyans soon recognised that the countries of the Soviet Bloc would not be willing to supply weapons to Libya without Moscow's consent. This fact was also pointed out to Gaddafi by the Egyptian leader Gamal Abdel Nasser. Therefore, it was decided to first arm only one mechanised infantry brigade and one armoured brigade with armament from communist states. At the same time, Gaddafi demanded that all training be carried out only by the Egyptians; the arrival of Soviet military advisors in Libya was out of the question.

However, if the Libyan leadership wanted to build an air defence system and set up three additional army brigades, it was necessary to negotiate directly with the Soviet Union. Left with no option, Gaddafi was forced to reconsider his stance on Moscow. On 23 February 1972, a Libyan-Egyptian delegation flew to the Soviet capital. During the negotiations, Libyan representatives invited top Soviet officials on a state visit to Libya. At the same time, a Soviet-Libyan agreement on friendship and cooperation was signed. However, when Soviet Prime Minister Alexei Kosygin and Iraqi President Ahmed Hassan al-Bakr signed an agreement on friendship and cooperation on 9 April 1972, an enraged Gaddafi cut diplomatic ties with Iraq and harshly criticised Iraqi Ba'athists. Moscow had lost hope that it could easily get Colonel Gaddafi on its side. Instead, the Libyan leader attacked the Soviet Union and communism in his speeches. Despite ideological contradictions, the Soviet Bloc led by Moscow did not resign from cooperation with Libya because it did not want to

Table 18: Known Czechoslovak arms export to Libya, 1970–1974[5]

Type	Number of examples	Year of delivery	Note
Sa 23 and Sa 25, 9mm submachine gun	2	1971	from the stocks of the Czechoslovak People's Army
	1	1973	from the stocks of the Czechoslovak People's Army
	1	1974	from the stocks of the Czechoslovak People's Army
vz. 61, 7.65mm submachine gun	1	1971	from the stocks of the Czechoslovak People's Army
vz. 52/57, 7.62mm rifle	1	1971	from the stocks of the Czechoslovak People's Army
vz. 52/57, 7.62mm machine gun	1	1971	from the stocks of the Czechoslovak People's Army
ammunition for small arms and tank machine guns	500	1970	from the stocks of the Czechoslovak People's Army
	3,153,200	1971	from the stocks of the Czechoslovak People's Army
T-55, medium tank	35	1971	newly manufactured
	42	1972	newly manufactured
	40	1973	newly manufactured
	154	1974	newly manufactured
T-55K, command tank	6	1972	newly manufactured
	10	1973	newly manufactured
	52	1974	newly manufactured
VT-55 (VT-55KS), armoured recovery vehicle	10	1971	newly manufactured
	2	1972	newly manufactured
	20	1974	newly manufactured
OT-62 TOPAS, armoured personnel carrier	43	1970 ?	probably from the stocks of the Czechoslovak People's Army
	57	1971	newly manufactured
PTDB, mobile tank workshop	1	1971	on Praga V3S chassis, from the stocks of the Czechoslovak People's Army

make room for competition from the West or the People's Republic of China.[6]

The opportunity to revise relations with the Soviet Union and its satellites came as a result of the October 1973 Arab-Israeli War. While the war was still raging, the Libyan government turned to Czechoslovakia with a request to deliver a large amount of military hardware. For this reason, on 13 October 1973, Libyan Prime Minister Major Abdessalam Jalloud met with Czechoslovak Ambassador Štefan Uher who then sent a dispatch to Prague the following day informing the Czechoslovak leadership of Libya's request for an urgent supply of weapons.

The Libyans demanded 300 T-55 tanks, which would be destined for Syria (150 examples) and Libya (remaining 150 examples). Together with the tanks, it was required to deliver all types of ammunition for the tank guns to the maximum extent possible. 'The deadline – the first ship'. Jalloud also asked for an 'unlimited number' of anti-tank guns with ammunition, as many anti-aircraft guns with ammunition as possible, and 40 MiG-21 fighters. He ended his list of requirements with words – 'prices do not matter'.[7]

HTS representative Miloslav Chocholouš with two Czechoslovak People's Army officers acting as technical consultants arrived in Tripoli on 18 October to hold respective business negotiations. The first meeting with high-ranking Libyan officers took place in the building of the General Staff of the Armed Forces of the Libyan Arab Republic the next day at 1:30 a.m. The Libyans were mostly interested in new T-55 tanks and MiG-21 aircraft. Additional negotiations followed during subsequent days. The last one was held in the afternoon on 24 October, one day before the end of the war. In the course of the last meeting, the Czechoslovak representatives confirmed Prague's readiness to offer immediate military assistance to Libya.[8]

Colonel Gaddafi was highly dissatisfied with the outcomes of the conflict. Not only did Egyptian President Anwar Sadat did not inform him about the intention of the Egyptian and Syrian armed forces to strike Israel but he did not allow Gaddafi to attend the meeting of the commanders-in-chief of the Arab militaries. The failure of the Egyptian offensive and subsequent ceasefire with Israel in January 1974 infuriated the Libyan leader. Gaddafi subsequently condemned Sadat's actions as treason.[9]

THE BEGINNING OF THE GOLDEN TIMES

Thus, in late January 1974, the Czechoslovak chargé d'affaires in Tripoli informed Prague about the Libyan intention to send a government delegation to Czechoslovakia for an official visit as soon as possible. Bilateral talks with a Libyan delegation led by Prime Minister Major Abdessalam Jalloud took place in Prague between 11 and 13 February 1974. Jalloud was received by General Secretary of the Central Committee of the Communist Party of Czechoslovakia (*Ústřední výbor Komunistické strany Československa*, ÚV KSČ) Gustáv Husák, and President Army General Ludvík Svoboda. He also held talks with Prime Minister Lubomír Štrougal. During negotiations with Czechoslovak officials, the Libyan Prime Minister apologised for Gaddafi's anti-Soviet and anti-communist assaults as a misunderstanding emerging from 'incomplete information'.

> Jalloud was very critical of current developments in Egypt, where right-wing forces are gaining ground by Egypt's transition from "Nasser and Nasserism" to the sphere of US influence. He expressed the belief that such an attitude could be stopped by further strengthening the relations of cooperation between socialist countries and Arab states. As for Libya's position, it is interested and determined to make every effort to get to know each other better and to strengthen cooperation with the Union of Soviet Socialist Republics and other socialist countries within the common front of the fight against imperialism, for socialism, for the elimination of exploitation. [...] Jalloud described possible misunderstandings in relations between Libya and the socialist countries as the result of hostile slander and propaganda that sought to break their natural alliance.

However, the primary purpose of Jalloud's visit to Czechoslovakia was not to interpret Libyan ideological flexibility but to buy Czechoslovak weapons. A special Czechoslovak-Libyan commission was set up to discuss the issue of arms supplies and military assistance, Colonel Hamed al-Belkas was appointed as head from the Libyan side and František Langer, the boss of the HTS, from the Czechoslovak side. The commission's meetings were

An Ilyushin Il-18B passenger aircraft of the Czechoslovak Airlines, seen at Prague International in the early 1970s. These aircraft were used in the late 1970s to transport Czechoslovak military advisors to Libya and back. (Martin Smisek collection)

concluded by the signing of a deal for the supply of 200 T-55 tanks during 1974 for approximately 581 million CSK under conditions of cash payment in hard currency.

Despite the massive production capacity of the Czechoslovak tank manufacturer Závody ťažkého strojárstva Martin, the latest Libyan demand caused quite a lot of problems:

The contract for the supply of 200 tanks, which was signed on the basis of a decision of the highest party and government bodies, made during the visit of the Libyan Prime Minister, creates a situation that Czechoslovak commitments for tank supplies in 1974 exceed production capabilities by 80 tanks. At the same time, Egypt's urgent demands are completely uncovered, and only 100 used tanks, released by the Federal Ministry of National Defence, are available for Syria's urgent demands. This creates a very difficult situation, for the solution of which it is recommended to adopt a corresponding resolution of the Presidium ÚV KSČ.

To supplement the information, it is stated that according to the report of the Libyan delegation, Poland offered delivery of 400 tanks by the first half of 1975 at better prices than the now achieved Czechoslovak prices.

In addition, a protocol was signed on 19 February 1974 which, based on Libyan requirements, expressed Czechoslovakia's willingness to assess and, where appropriate, provide assistance in the following areas:

- construction of a tank manufacturing plant,
- construction of a plant for the production of spare parts for the T-55 tanks,
- construction of a plant for the production of tank and artillery ammunition,
- construction of several plants for the repairs of tanks and armoured personnel carriers,
- construction of a plant for the repairs of infantry and artillery armament (calibres ranging from 7.62mm to 122mm),
- establishment of a tank technical school.

Moreover, Prague had promised to consider an urgent Libyan demand for the delivery of an additional 600 T-55 tanks during 1975.[10]

While T-55 tanks from Czechoslovak license production continued to flow into the inventory of the Libyan Arab Army in the next years, Libyan demands for the construction of production, repair, and school facilities were rejected or the need for technical clarification by experts from both parties was pointed out. The request to build a tank plant was rejected for the second time. In June 1972, during a meeting of František Langer in Tripoli, representatives of the Libyan armed forces expressed a request for the construction of a plant for the production of T-55 tanks. Although Prague had strong doubts about the feasibility of such a proposition, in October 1972 a Czechoslovak technical group was sent to Libya in this regard. However, eventually, negotiations on technical issues did not take place because the Libyans were not able to establish a group of qualified experts who would be able to discuss this project competently. The most important aspect was whether Moscow would give its consent to the transfer of license for the tank production to Libya. The whole matter was resolved in April 1973, when the HTS received a clearly negative Soviet response.[11]

Therefore, negotiations on the construction of armoured vehicle repair plants in Tobruk, Tripoli, and Benghazi had made the most

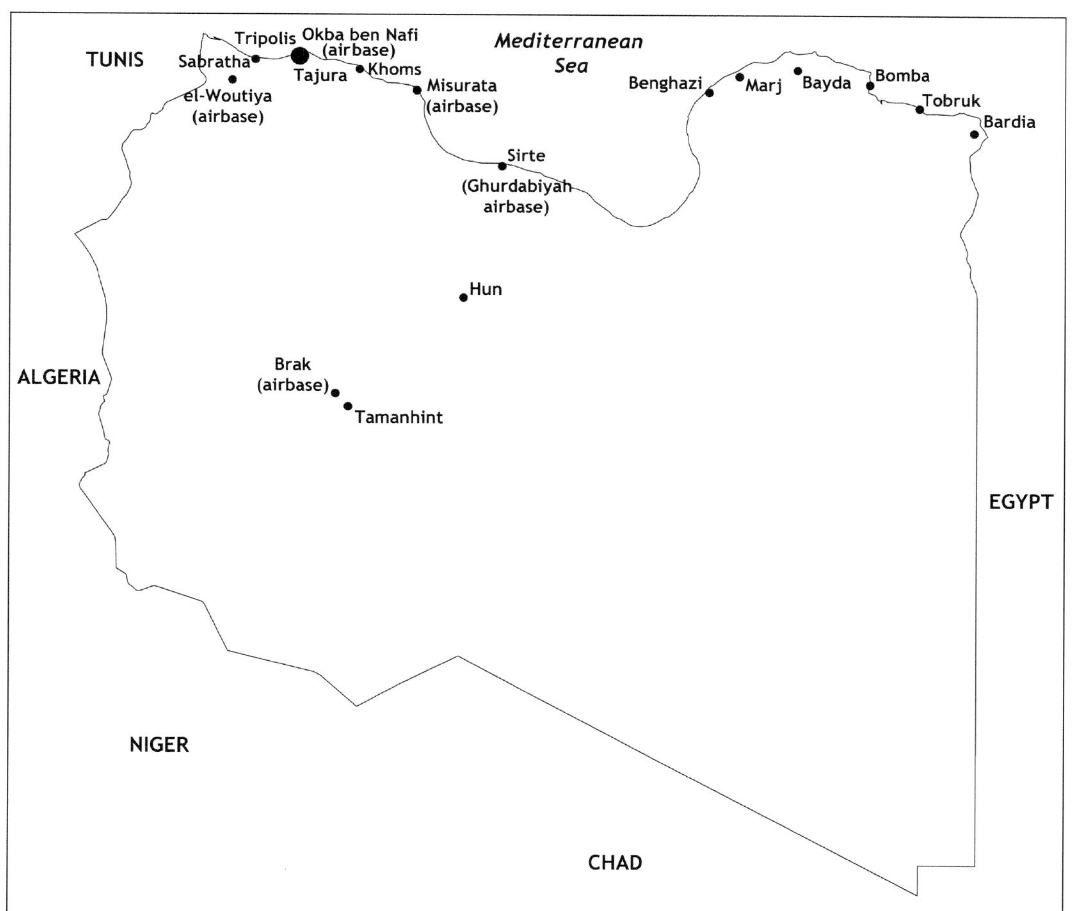

Map of places in Libya mentioned in text and related to the deliveries of arms and military facilities, as well as the activity of the Czechoslovak military advisors and specialists. (Map by b.b.h.illustrations)

progress. In the end, while the Soviets took over the responsibility of constructing of these facilities at Tripoli and Benghazi, Prague continued in the project in Tobruk. Libya had secured the construction of the buildings and facilities itself. Czechoslovakia supplied the necessary machinery and technical equipment and ensured its installation on site. Czechoslovak advisors subsequently ensured the start-up of this repair plant.[12]

In the end, most other projects demanded by the Libyans could not be implemented due to Moscow's disapproval. Besides this, Tripoli was interested in the local production of infantry weapons. Hence, Czechoslovakia provided the study for the license production of vz. 61 submachine guns, vz. 58 assault rifles, and vz. 59 general purpose machine guns. The documentation was handed over to the Libyan representatives in late 1973 through the business department of the Czechoslovak embassy in Tripoli. In 1975, the HTS sold to Libya manufacturing documentation for all three types. Despite this, the license production of Czechoslovak small arms was never initiated in Libya.[13]

Nevertheless, the Czechoslovak infantry weapons found their way into the inventory of Libyan armed and security forces. In 1981, OMNIPOL delivered 20,000 vz. 58 assault rifles.

THE T-55: LIBYAN BESTSELLER

As soon as the contract for 200 T-55 tanks was signed, further negotiations continued in Prague between 2 and 8 May 1974 regarding the delivery of another 600 tanks. During the talks, the Libyan delegation further increased the required number of tanks. Before the negotiations, Prague decided to offer Libya 600 tanks in 1975 and 200 the following year. Finally, during negotiations with the Libyans, the HTS officials agreed to deliver a total of 720 tanks, 460 of which were to be delivered in 1975 and the remaining 260 in the first quarter of 1976. The Libyan delegation categorically demanded acceptance of the previous price, for tanks already imported into Libya – 353,430 DM (3,019,988 CSK) for one vehicle.

The contract included the delivery of a total of 720 tanks, of which 480 of the basic combat variant, 210 of the command version, and 30 of the recovery variant. The contract also included the delivery of spare parts amounting to 20 % of the total financial value of the contract. The deal was signed on 7 May 1974 and its overall value reached 306,858,240 DM (2,622,042,240 CSK).

Table 19: Contracted shipments of T-55 tanks for Libya, 1974–1976[14]

Supplier	Delivery time		
	1974	1975	1976
Poland	120	331	-
Czechoslovakia	200	460	260
Soviet Union	200 – 220		-

The two contracts for a total of 920 T-55 tanks in different versions were worth 377 million DM (more than 3 billion CSK). Up to August 1975, Czechoslovakia supplied Libya with 667 T-55 medium tanks, 302 T-55K command tanks, and 62 VT-55 armoured recovery vehicles together with related spare parts. Moreover, Czechoslovak arms factories manufactured for Libya 7.5 million rounds of 7.62mm NATO ammunition.

All deliveries of tanks resulting from the last two contracts were completed according to the agreed schedule – in the first quarter of 1976. By this time, Libya had received a total of 1,065 tanks from Czechoslovakia. Deliveries of related tank spare parts worth 42 million DM (approximately 350 million CSK) were completed in April 1977. From the start of deliveries of military hardware to Libya in 1970 up to 1976, Tripoli spent more than 4 billion CSK on Czechoslovak weapons, which were paid for in cash and hard currency.

According to Resolution No. 119 of the Czechoslovak government from 2 May 1974, the HTS concluded on 7 May 1975 General Contract No. 43520 with the Libyans, containing framework conditions for the training of Libyan military personnel at the facilities of the Federal Ministry of National Defence and the Federal Ministry of General Mechanical Engineering. On 27 August 1975, the Czechoslovak government approved in Resolution No. 233

T-55s of the Libyan Arab Army at a military parade in Tripoli, in the late 1970s. These tanks were supplied to Libya not only from Czechoslovakia, but also from Poland and the Soviet Union. (Martin Smisek collection)

Colonel General Karel Rusov (right), chief of the Czechoslovak General Staff, seen during a visit to Libya in 1974. (via Martin Smisek)

some Libyan requirements for military training. Subsequently, a deal was signed with Libya to send the first trainees to the Czechoslovak Socialist Republic. Thus, 96 Libyans were accepted for instruction in the medium and general overhaul of T-55 tanks and OT-62 armoured personnel carriers.[15] The training itself was preceded by a language school where the trainees learned English. However, all Libyan students were recalled to their homeland prematurely in early 1976. 'The reason was the then domestic political situation in Libya.'[16]

ASSESSMENT FROM THE CZECHOSLOVAK EMBASSY: 1976

Despite the procurement of a massive quantity of military hardware, the overall combat capability of the Armed Forces of the Libyan Arab Republic in 1976 was still poor which was reflected in the analysis prepared by the Czechoslovak embassy in Tripoli:

The main shortcoming of the Libyan armed forces is insufficient combat training and a complete lack of qualified personnel, especially with adequate technical education. For this reason, a number of foreign advisors work in the Libyan Arab Republic to maintain and operate demanding modern technology. For example, Mirage aircraft are mostly piloted by Pakistani pilots who are, among other things, rotated at relatively short intervals, thus providing Pakistan with combat training for its own pilots.

As a result of the rift between the Libyan Arab Republic and the Arab Republic of Egypt, about 4,000 Egyptian advisors working in the Libyan armed forces were recalled by President Sadat in 1974. However, after an unsuccessful attempt to overthrow Gaddafi in August last year, in which Egyptian intelligence reportedly played a significant role, a number of Egyptian advisors reportedly returned and some of them even work directly in military staffs.

The basic problem of the Libyan armed forces remains the use of a relatively large amount of imported expensive military hardware which becomes obsolete morally and physically through storage and unprofessional maintenance. To illustrate this, it is possible to give an example where, in relation to an estimated number of 26,000 members of the ground forces, a total of about 2,600 tanks have been imported in recent years. The Libyan leadership is buying so many weapons with the intention

of supplying them, if necessary, to other countries, especially Arab countries, in order to achieve political benefits and at the same time reduce their dependence on states producing the weapons in question. An example of this is the material and military assistance provided by the Libyan Arab Republic to Egypt and Syria during the 1973 Ramadan War. This year, Libya also provided an unspecified amount of weapons to the People's Democratic Republic of Algeria in its dispute with Morocco over the territory of the former Western Sahara, which were transported by the West German crew of the Libyan ship "Ghat". Nevertheless, the vast majority of purchased military hardware remains unused, and there are growing critical remarks among the public about excessive military spending.[17]

TRIPOLI IS REPLACING CAIRO

The Libyan interest in deliveries of military hardware from Czechoslovakia did not subside in the following period either. From 13 to 15 October 1975, the Czechoslovak Prime Minister Lubomír Štrougal paid an official visit to Libya. His welcome and stay were spectacular.

The high reception and attention received by the Czechoslovak prime minister in Libya, as well as the good results of talks and negotiations with Libyan leaders, testify to the progressive positive development of the Libyan leadership, its rapprochement with the countries of the socialist community, led by the Soviet Union, and a growing interest in mutually beneficial cooperation.

[…] The Libyan party paid special attention to the welcome of the Prime Minister of Czechoslovakia and his entourage. The arrival was attended by Prime Minister Jalloud, 12 ministers, other senior public officials, the army leadership, headed by the Chief of the General Staff, and the head of all foreign embassies in Tripoli. The Libyan party promptly obtained a picture of General Secretary and President of the Republic comrade G Husák and decorated the liveliest places in Tripoli with them. The Czechoslovak delegation was welcomed by the population on the way from the airport, the route was decorated with Czechoslovak flags.

As usual, the main topics of the negotiations included the supply of Czechoslovak weapons: 'Gaddafi expressed his full consent to the all-round development of mutual relations and cooperation and, like Jalloud, showed great interest in the supply of special material'. Libyan officials called on the Czechoslovak representatives not to provide any more weapons in the future to Egypt which, according to the Libyans, had already clearly sided with the United States. The Czechoslovak delegation diplomatically rejected the Libyan demand, referring to contractual obligations. In fact, Egypt was Czechoslovakia's most important business partner within the Third World in 1975 and disruptions in the military area could bring vast repercussions with severe financial losses.

On the other hand, the situation on the international scene developed in favour of Tripoli. Growing tensions between the Soviet Union and Egypt led Moscow to cut back on shipments of armament to Egypt in early 1975 and to halt them completely in the second half of the same year. Upon Soviet pressure, Prague followed the line and stopped arms supplies as well.[18]

As a result, Colonel Gaddafi became not only the main client in the Third World but also the best paying customer of Czechoslovak weapons in the coming decade.

Libya's relations with the countries of the socialist community in the military sector deepened significantly after the visit of Colonel Gaddafi to Moscow in December 1976 and Major Jalloud to the Czechoslovak Socialist Republic, the People's Republic of Bulgaria, and the Socialist Federal Republic of Yugoslavia in May of this year [1977]. This was reflected both in public speeches by the main Libyan statesmen and in concrete negotiations aimed at improving the combat capability of the Libyan armed forces with the help of socialist countries. If the previous military aid of the countries of the socialist community was concentrated mainly in the supply of armament, especially for the ground forces, then the Libyan side is currently asking the countries of the socialist community for the supply of fighter jets, missiles, and construction of weapons and ammunition plants, as well as great assistance in education and training of technical and command staff of all kinds. This is evidenced not only by the protocols that Libya has signed with the countries of the socialist community in the military sector but also by very intensive negotiations to specify the content of the protocols this year.

Continued tensions in Libyan-Egyptian relations, the continuing possibility of a repeat of the attack by the Egyptian armed forces against Libya with the support of Sudan and Chad, and the decision of the Libyan leadership to fully support the national liberation struggle of the Arab and African states are leading to the rapid increase of Libya's defence capabilities.[19]

Table 20: Financial value of the Czechoslovak arms deliveries to Libya and related military assistance, 1970-1977[20]

Year	Value (million USD)
1970	54.4
1971	232.8
1972	176.8
1973	178.8
1974	715.2
1975	1,767.3
1976	746.7
1977	38.3 (as of 31 August)

A T-55 of the Libyan Arab Army seen during a military parade in the early 1980s. (Martin Smisek collection)

PROTOCOL FROM 17 MAY 1977

Thanks to rising profits from the sale of oil, the Libyan leadership was able to afford to buy huge quantities of weapons. This, of course, greatly pleased the communists in Prague who, with the hard currency gained by selling weapons to Libya, could buy selected goods and raw materials in the West since these commodities were unavailable in the Soviet Bloc.

A substantial intensification of Czechoslovak-Libyan military relations took place in 1977. First, between 18 and 24 April, the General Director of the HTS František Langer held talks in Tripoli with representatives of the Libyan Ministry of Defence on the prospect of further mutual relations in the field of military cooperation. The Libyans came forward with a request for further deliveries of Czechoslovak armament. Libyan demands were more than welcome in Prague since, as an official document for the Presidium ÚV KSČ (*Předsednictvo ÚV KSČ*) noted: 'After the stagnation of exports of our special material, which manifested itself in 1976, Libya is practically the only developing country that is willing to accept on a large scale the special material that is produced in the Czechoslovak Socialist Republic, in cash payment in hard currency'.

A Dassault Mirage 5D fighter-bomber of the Libyan Arab Air Force, seen in the mid-1970s, before their serial numbers applied in Arabic digits were re-applied in Persian digits in the aftermath of the short war between Egypt and Libya. (Albert Grandolini collection)

A further bilateral meeting took place in Prague from 16 to 17 May 1977. The Libyan delegation led by Abdessalam Jalloud further expanded and clarified the requirements for shipments of Czechoslovak arms:

During the negotiations, the Libyan side indicated the interconnectedness and dependence of all its requirements and conditioned the implementation of an extraordinary volume of material supplies by the Czechoslovak Socialist Republic providing Libya with the required technical assistance by sending several hundred Czechoslovak military instructors to Libya and possibly training Libyan personnel in the Czechoslovak Socialist Republic.

On the other hand, the extraordinary scope of Libyan requirements, including the need for a quick and comprehensive solution, will require extraordinary measures to be taken by all Czechoslovak participating ministries due to the Libyan side's demands on the exact fulfilment of obligations in terms and quality, as even partial non-fulfilment of assumed obligations is associated with severe financial penalties.

From the economic point of view, this is an extraordinary opportunity to achieve a significant foreign exchange benefit for the Czechoslovak national economy under the most advantageous payment conditions.

On 17 May, the talks resulted in the signing of the Protocol covering Libya's massive requirements in the sphere of arms deliveries from the Czechoslovak Socialist Republic, including military assistance. According to the Protocol signed by Prime Minister Lubomír Štrougal, Prague agreed to carry out:

- deliveries of multiple rocket launchers, tanks, armoured support vehicles, infantry fighting vehicles, training aircraft, and ammunition,
- construction and establishment of military repair facilities, ammunition plants, and an arms factory,
- military assistance by sending more than 1,000 instructors, military advisors, and technical experts.[21]

The overall value of all Libyan requirements reached more than 3 billion CSK (ca 200 million USD).

Table 21: Czechoslovak commitments according to the Protocol from 17 May 1977[22]

Item	Commitment	Description
1	Establishment of an air force training school	Submission of a bid for project, equipment, curricula, documentation, sending of instructor pilots, and construction of buildings for an air force training school with three years of teaching with a capacity of 300 to 400 students per year. On 21 July 1977, the Libyans put forward their decision to postpone this project by two to three years.
2	Deliveries of L-39 Albatros training aircraft	Libya demanded the accelerated delivery of 16 aircraft and the additional delivery of another 48 airplanes for the training of pilots and technicians at the existing air force training facility, together with a bid for training programmes and the deployment of instructors.
3	Establishment of a technical centre	Libya requested a bid for a technical centre to train aircraft technicians to operate, maintain, and repair aircraft with a capacity of 300 to 400 students per year at three years of instruction. On 21 July 1977, the Libyans put forward their decision to postpone this project by two to three years.
4	Training on MiG-21 fighters	Czechoslovakia and Libya considered the possibility of eventual training of Libyan personnel on MiG-21 aircraft.
5	Delivery of multiple rocket launchers	Libya demanded the delivery of four complete rocket launcher battalions equipped with 80 (72 operational and 8 reserve) vz. 70 GRAD multiple rocket launchers.
6	Delivery of armoured support vehicles	Libya requested the shipment of 50 MT-55 armoured vehicle-launched bridges and 50 JVBT-55 armoured crane vehicles.
7	Delivery of tanks	Libya demanded the delivery of 250 T-55 tanks.
9	Delivery of spare parts for T-55 tanks	
9	Delivery of infantry fighting vehicles	Libya requested the delivery of 250 BVP-1 infantry fighting vehicles.
10	Delivery of a tank simulator	Libya requested the delivery of one TT-55 simulator for tank drivers.
11	A medium tank repair facility	
12	Establishment of a communication centre	Facility for the training of Libyan signal personnel.
13	Project for the storage of heavy spare parts for tanks and armoured vehicles	
14	Construction of a plant for the production of infantry weapons	
15	Construction of a plant for the production of ammunition for infantry weapons	
16	Construction of a plant for the production of artillery ammunition (medium and large calibres)	

Item	Commitment	Description
17	Technical assistance for vz. 70 GRAD multiple rocket launchers	
18	10 complete instructor crews for vz. 70 GRAD multiple rocket launchers	
19	25 specialists – warehousemen for the storage of spare parts of armoured vehicles	
20	Two mechanical engineers – advisors for the management of a tank repair plant	
21	10 headmen for repairs of tanks	
22	Two technicians – experts on repairs of stabilisers and tank turrets	
23	100 complete instructor crews for the operation and maintenance of T-55 tanks	
24	Six technicians for medium overhauls of M-46 guns	
25	Six technicians for medium overhauls of vz. 70 GRAD multiple rocket launchers	
26	Two technicians for repairs of artillery optical devices	
27	10 complete instructor crews for M-46 guns	
28	Deliveries of T-72 tanks	Libya expressed a wish to receive T-72 tanks as soon as Czechoslovakia begins their license production.

As expected, the extent of Czechoslovakia's commitments required a blessing from Moscow: 'The exceptional nature of the mentioned requirements, their economic scope, and political importance require, in view of the obligations under the signed Protocol, to carry out an expedited consultation in the Union of Soviet Socialist Republics at the appropriate governmental or party level'.

Wasting no time, HTS boss František Langer unofficially consulted on this matter in Moscow with his counterpart General Sergeychik (Chief of the Main Engineering Administration of the State Committee of the Council of Ministers of the Union of Soviet Socialist Republics for Foreign Economic Relations) on 19 and 20 May 1977. The negotiations showed that the Libyans turned to the Soviet Union, Yugoslavia, and some other countries of the Soviet Bloc with similar demands as well.[23]

The main supplier of military hardware to Tripoli at the time was the Soviet Union which provided guns, tanks, missile technology, air defence systems, and combat aircraft. The second in line was Czechoslovakia. Poland mainly delivered tanks (up to August 1977 a total of more than 1,000 examples) and related spare parts. In addition, it carried out the construction of various military facilities. At the same time, it tried to sell its TS-11 Iskra training aircraft. Bulgaria supplied Libya mainly with tank and artillery ammunition and small arms. Bulgarian companies also built several military installations. Yugoslavia established an air force academy in Misurata and provided the necessary specialists and instructors, together with SOKO G-2A Galeb jet trainers and J-21 Jastreb light attack aircraft. On the other hand, the involvement of East Germany was minimal. Around 1977, it had only begun to make efforts to supply medical and logistic equipment, infantry weapons, and related ammunition.[24]

The Libyan and Egyptian disputes escalated into a short border war that lasted from 21 to 24 July 1977. During the May negotiations in Prague, the Libyans again openly asked the top-level Czechoslovak officials to suspend tank deliveries to Egypt. Due to the Soviet-Egyptian split, the contract from the summer of 1975 for the supply of 220 T-55 tanks for the Egyptian Army from Czechoslovakia was significantly reduced. Therefore, the Czechoslovak representatives were free to assure the Libyans that no further arms deals with Egypt were planned in the future. The T-55 tanks were to be imported preferentially to Libya.[25]

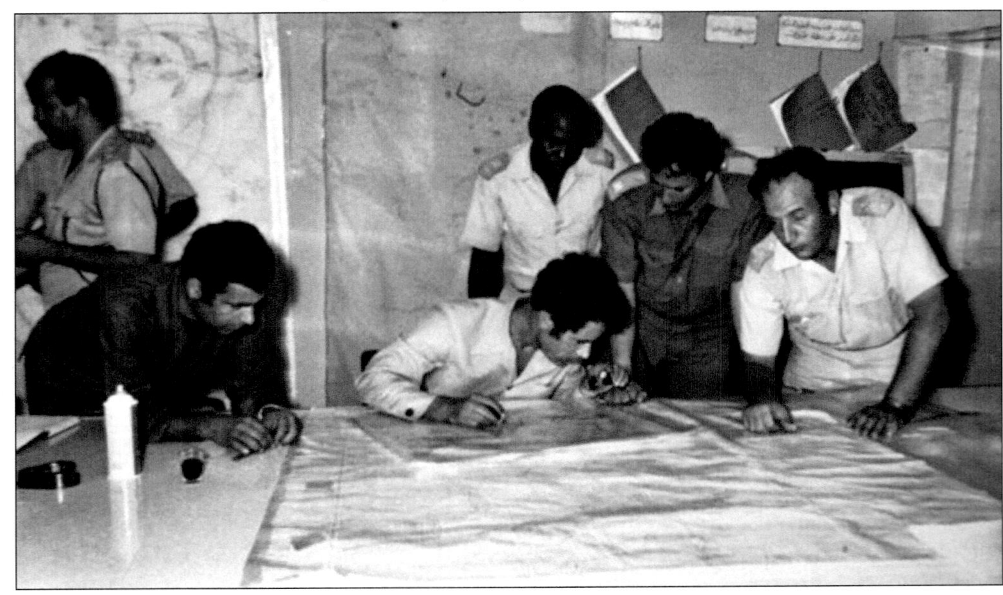

Gaddafi in his war room during the short war with Egypt, in July 1977. (Martin Smisek collection)

CZECHOSLOVAK GRADS FOR GADDAFI

The promise to sell four rocket launcher battalions was confirmed by the Czechoslovak government in Resolution No. 136 on 16 June 1977. Correspondingly, the HTS and the Libyan Ministry of Defence concluded Contract No. 21-7-82 in August 1977 which covered the delivery of 80 vz. 70 GRAD multiple rocket launchers (eight of them were reserve) with related spare parts and almost all needed support equipment. The only exception was ammunition vehicles because the Libyans refused to order a variant of the Praga V3S which was used as standard in the Czechoslovak People's Army (*Československá lidová armáda*). Instead, the Libyans intended to order separately 144 ammunition trucks based on the Tatra 813 chassis. According to the terms of the deal, the hardware for the first rocket launcher battalion was to be delivered by the end of 1977.

As a result, Libya became the second export user of vz. 70 GRAD multiple rocket launchers after East Germany. Since the contract stipulated the delivery of some equipment of Soviet origin (most importantly UAZ-452T topographic survey vehicles, VR-2M wind speed measuring devices, and PUO-9M fire control devices), Moscow's consent was absolutely necessary. Prime Minister Alexei Kosygin gave such approval to his Czechoslovak counterpart Lubomír Štrougal: 'As for the supply of UAZ-452T survey vehicles, PUO-9 fire control devices, and VR-2 wind speed measuring devices to Libya in accordance with the contract signed by the foreign trade organisations of the Czechoslovak Socialist Republic and Libya in August 1977, there are no objections on our part'.

However, this answer did not come until 28 November 1978, so that the required equipment was not delivered to Libya until the first half of 1979. This meant that the delivery deadlines set by the contract were not met. The Libyans, meanwhile, complained bitterly and urged 'the fulfilment of contractual obligations at various levels and argued that the combat capabilities of the supplied battalions were being undermined'.[26]

Table 22: The delivery of four rocket launcher battalions (Contract No. 21-7-82), 1977–1979[27]

Type	Number of examples	Note
vz. 70 GRAD, multiple rocket launcher	80	39 vehicles delivered from the stocks of the Czechoslovak People's Army (18 in 1977 and 21 in 1978)
122-JROF-RM70, 122mm high explosive rocket	95,640	23,000 rockets delivered from the stocks of the Czechoslovak People's Army (8,000 in 1977 and 15,000 in 1978)
122 JROF-Šk-RM70, training round	160	for the training of loading and unloading of the multiple rocket launcher
UAZ-452T, topographic survey vehicle	4	from the stocks of the Czechoslovak People's Army
command vehicle	4	on Praga V3S chassis
mobile artillery workshop	4	on Praga V3S chassis, one vehicle delivered from the stocks of the Czechoslovak People's Army in the PDD version, remaining vehicles probably delivered in the same standard
PAD-1M, mobile car workshop	8	on Praga V3S chassis, from the stocks of the Czechoslovak People's Army
BZ T-813, dozer blade for vz. 70 GRAD	27	
vz. 60, compass	120	from the stocks of the Czechoslovak People's Army
D-6, artillery binoculars	80	from the stocks of the Czechoslovak People's Army
AST, periscopic telescope	20	from the stocks of the Czechoslovak People's Army
TZK, telescope	20	from the stocks of the Czechoslovak People's Army
VR-2M, wind speed measuring device	16	from the stocks of the Czechoslovak People's Army
Metra 950, anemometer	16	from the stocks of the Czechoslovak People's Army
PUO-9M, fire control device	20	from the stocks of the Czechoslovak People's Army
OEM-2, rangefinder	8	from the stocks of the Czechoslovak People's Army
PAB-2A, artillery periscopic compass	40	from the stocks of the Czechoslovak People's Army
T-60, theodolite	4	from the stocks of the Czechoslovak People's Army
PNV-57, night vision goggles for drivers	80	from the stocks of the Czechoslovak People's Army
camouflage net	80 sets	

One of the lessons Gaddafi drew from the October 1973 Arab-Israeli War was that his country needed huge stocks of reserve weaponry. Correspondingly, much of the arms and equipment acquired by Libya in the 1970s was stored immediately following delivery. The same was true for a number of vz. 70 GRAD multiple rocket launchers acquired from Czechoslovakia. This pair was photographed during one of many military parades held in Tripoli in the 1970s. (Albert Grandolini collection)

FROM CZECHOSLOVAKIA WITH LOVE: TANKS, MISSILES, AND RECOILLESS GUNS

At the same time as rocket launchers, deliveries of other military hardware from Czechoslovakia to Libya continued. Between November 1977 and January 1978, four cargo ships loaded with Czechoslovak armament sailed from the Yugoslav port of Ploče to Tripoli. They transported not only 18 vz. 70 GRAD multiple rocket launchers, related ammunition, and other equipment for one rocket launcher battalion but also 20 T-55 tanks, 30 JVBT-55 armoured crane vehicles, and 28 MT-55 armoured vehicle-launched bridges.[28]

When Czechoslovak Minister of Foreign Affairs Bohuslav Chňoupek visited Libya in December 1977, in official talks with Prime Minister Jalloud, the issue of Czechoslovak arms supplies was discussed as usual. On that occasion, Chňoupek complained about payments for the Czechoslovak 'special deliveries which Libya currently pays by transfer from its regular bank account in the Federal Republic of Germany. He pointed out that such a form is often lengthy and, in addition, provides the Federal Republic of Germany with information on the scope of our contacts. Jalloud did not respond to this remark'.[29]

The shipments from Czechoslovakia included RPG-75 single-shot anti-tank weapons, 9K11 Malyutka (NATO reporting name AT-3 Sagger) portable anti-tank guided missile systems, and vz. 59 recoilless guns as well. In 1977, Prague delivered 1,500 RPG-75s to Libya, the identical number of the same weapons was ordered by Libyans in late March 1978. This time, Tripoli demanded an expedited delivery within 7 to 10 days by air. Prague duly complied with Libyan wishes. The required number of RPG-75s was loaded on an aircraft of Czechoslovak Airlines (*Československé aerolinie*) on 22 April 1978. Moreover, up to 1979, Libya bought 9K11 Malyutka systems with 1,080 9M14M anti-tank guided missiles that were manufactured in Czechoslovakia under license.

The first 50 vz. 59 recoilless guns were delivered to Libya in the third quarter of 1977. The unloading of these guns and related equipment was completed in Libyan ports on 10 September 1977. However, the training could not follow immediately thereafter as

originally planned because the Libyans did not provide students nor relevant training equipment. After a series of negotiations and the intervention of an HTS representative in Libya at higher echelons of the Libyan Arab Army, the training began only on 25 September 1977. Up to then, Libyan officials changed the start date several times. Meanwhile, the Czechoslovak instructor team processed the necessary translations and reproduced the documentation on the basic characteristics and functions of the guns which were handed over to the customer.

In order for the training to take place at all, the Czechoslovak instructors had to choose the necessary equipment for the instruction in the warehouse. The live firing originally planned for 29 September had to be postponed until 1 and 2 October 1977, due to bad weather and the inability of the Libyans to provide the necessary ammunition. Therefore, the training took place in the period from 25 September to 4 October 1977. During this time, trainees were trained in basic technical and firing tasks needed for the fire from the guns, including safety guidelines for shooting. A total of 40 Libyan soldiers were trained in the operation of vz. 59 guns. During the training course, they took turns operating all the gun's functions and personally carried out live firing.

On 7 March 1978, the director of the OS-20 business team from the HTS turned to the Federal Ministry of National Defence with a request for the accelerated delivery of 20 vz. 59 guns from the warehouses of the Czechoslovak People's Army. These weapons, together with spare parts and 3,200 rounds of ammunition, were dispatched from Czechoslovakia in May 1978.[30]

TOBRUK TANK REPAIR FACILITY

Meanwhile, Czechoslovakia dispatched its military and technical experts to Libya to put the repair facility for armoured vehicles at Tobruk into operation. This installation, known as Workshop No. 3, was established with Czechoslovak assistance. The company INPRO Praha played the role of the main supplier that provided the required technical equipment in cooperation with the Repair Plant 026 (*Opravárenský závod 026*).

Czechoslovak-manufactured VT-55s, OT-62s, and JVBT-55s seen at a military depot after the fall of the Gaddafi regime in 2011. (via Martin Smisek)

On 7 May 1975, OMNIPOL and the Ministry of Defence of the Libyan Arab Republic concluded Contract No. 43521 for technical assistance needed to set Workshop No. 3 into motion. The financial value of the deal reached 842,528.25 DM. A team of 15 specialists from Repair Plant 026, led by Jiří Tylšer, arrived in Libya in April 1977. Czechoslovak advisors served at Tobruk for 10 months and during their stay, they supervised the installation of the delivered machinery and then introduced overhauls of not only T-54 and T-55 tanks but also of OT-62 and BTR-60PB armoured personnel carriers. At the same time, they trained local personnel in the repair of these vehicles.

The Czechoslovak involvement in the operation of Workshop No. 3 was prolonged thanks to Supplement No. 1 of Contract No. 43521 which was awarded in March 1978. The value of this deal was 1,041,364.90 DM. Accordingly, a new team of 13 technical specialists and two interpreters under the leadership of Stanislav Zdobnický started the activities at Tobruk on 31 July 1978. The advisory team was a part of the Czechoslovak military training contingent deployed at that time to Libya and used the cover name Group T (Group No. 8). The members of this team returned to Czechoslovakia on 2 August 1979.

During their stay in Libya, Czechoslovak specialists performed medium and general overhauls of 104 vehicles in Workshop No. 3 (41 BTR-60PB armoured personnel carriers, 38 T-55 tanks, 19 BRDM-2 armoured scout cars, five VT-55 armoured recovery vehicles, and one BTR-50PK armoured personnel carrier). In addition, they repaired one D-30 howitzer. Based on special customer requirements, the group performed technical inspections and service repairs of 110 vehicles in military camps outside Tobruk: 53 T-55 tanks in Camp of 28 March, 29 BTR-60PB armoured personnel carriers in Camp Hamia, 17 T-55 tanks in Camp Bomba, and 11 BRDM-2 armoured scout cars in Camp Bardia. Also, Czechoslovak technicians overhauled two engines for the BTR-60PB, designed and manufactured 250 hedgehog barriers, repaired the electrical system and partially repaired hulls of nine BTR-60PBs and one BRDM-2. They also produced a model of a mine, designed and manufactured a prototype of a grenade launcher and performed its functional tests. At the same time, they established the production of small, scarce spare parts. In other cases, the lack of spare parts was compensated by dismantling components from written-off or unrepairable vehicles.

The customer, specifically the workshop commander, Captain Abdunabi, created very good conditions for the activities of the group of Czechoslovak experts in Tobruk. With his high professional and organisational skills, he ensured that the group could work evenly and with quality. He has a personal role in creating very good and friendly relations between Czechoslovak experts and members of the Libyan army working in the repair shop.[31]

ASSESSMENT FROM THE CZECHOSLOVAK EMBASSY: 1978

Officials from the Czechoslovak embassy in Tripoli continuously followed the situation in the Libyan Arab Armed Forces, which they described in May 1978 as follows:

The Libyan armed forces have undergone many changes since the 1969 Revolution, both in terms of personnel and in terms of military doctrine and the level of their combat capability. The original orientation towards Great Britain and Western states was gradually changed, the basis of the building became the principles of the Arab Republic of Egypt. The officers of the royal regime were in most cases discharged from the armed forces and replaced by young men, most of whom underwent training at a military training school in Benghazi or Egypt. At the same time, officers were sent for training to Western countries, the United States, Arab countries, and countries of the Indian subcontinent. This way of personnel training carries its problems in the application of different doctrines and different ways of training troops, organisations, and their use. The departure of Egyptian officers after the rift further complicated the situation in the Libyan army command.

The current command is not able to centrally control the troops and firmly command, especially in situations where often the most modern hardware was purchased abroad. Command remains largely decentralised, and commanders of individual military bases, often very young and inexperienced, have considerable authority and decide independently at their own discretion.

Despite considerable problems in mastering the command and control of troops, the armed forces remain a firm pillar of the current regime and play a crucial role in the exercise of political power.

The overall situation of command and control of troops is to be gradually resolved, on the one hand, with the help of military experts on the spot at military units and, on the other hand, the deployment of medium-level and senior-level military personnel to military schools of predominantly socialist countries. These trained commanders are then to ensure structural changes in the organisation of the army so that the armed forces are prepared to perform the country's existing tasks.

[…]

The leadership of the armed forces is young, weakly prepared to lead troops, and is technically unable to handle existing, often state-of-the-art military hardware purchased abroad, and to use it thoroughly. The command of the armed forces is aware of this situation and therefore with the purchase of military hardware abroad, technical assistance and training of personnel are provided so that the purchased equipment remains combat-ready even when it is not used.

This is the case of tanks and armoured vehicles, for which training, operation, and storage are provided by experts from the Czechoslovak Socialist Republic, the Union of Soviet Socialist Republics, the Polish People's Republic, and the Socialist Federal Republic of Yugoslavia. Armoured vehicles purchased in France, Brazil, and Great Britain are maintained in operational condition by the technicians of these countries. It also happens that laser sights are mounted on Czechoslovak tanks by experts from Great Britain.

In artillery, the hardware is also supplied mainly by socialist countries with appropriate services and training in employment. An exception is the 155mm self-propelled gun, where the training is carried out by experts from the Federal Republic of Germany and the technical operation is provided by experts from Italy. There is also a combination of Western and socialist technology. For example, Soviet surface-to-air missiles are mounted on chassis from the Federal Republic of Germany. Both parties provide services. Anti-tank missiles supplied by the Union of Soviet Socialist Republics and France are maintained in operational condition by experts from both countries. The surface-to-surface missile technology is exclusively in the hands of the supplier the Union of Soviet Socialist Republics.

The engineer equipment is mainly supplied from Great Britain and it provides service and training of technicians in Great Britain. The engineer school in Benghazi also uses technicians from Great Britain.

The communication technology, except for devices mounted directly in respective systems, is mainly from the Federal Republic of Germany, Great Britain. These are the means of communication used in NATO. The Federal Republic of Germany is currently building a communication system in the armed forces. Together with Western countries, Chinese experts and specialists from Taiwan are also involved in the use and operation.

Automobiles in the Libyan army [are] mainly of Western origin, especially from the Federal Republic of Germany, both freight and passenger transport in the army.

The air force is still dominated by Western technology, especially the French Mirage. The Libyan air force still has the largest number of them. Their operation is provided mainly by Pakistani and partly by French technicians. Most patrol flights are performed by Pakistani pilots. French and Italian helicopters are also serviced by technicians from both countries, the pilots are locals. Hercules military transport aircraft are still in the technical care of factory technicians from the USA.

Of the Soviet aircraft, the MiG-23 and Tu-22 are mainly used. They are mostly assembled on-site in Libya, they are still in the hands of Soviet experts.

In terms of airport support equipment, such as guidance and communication systems, they are also a combination of technology from Great Britain, the USA, France, and now Soviet devices are also gaining ground.

The training of air force officers is carried out at the air force academy in Misurata on Yugoslav material and by Yugoslav instructors. The training of non-commissioned officers, pilots, and technicians is carried out at the Okba air base near Tripoli (former Wheelus Field) by Czechoslovak experts on the basis of Czechoslovak syllabuses and equipment.

Soviet technology is being introduced into Libya's air defence system under the guidance and control of Soviet instructors. Some previously introduced devices are also used as part of the system.

The navy is currently using old warships. However, it is already equipped with coastal vessels with rockets and guided missiles of British and French origin.

Most commanders have not yet been able to command the units in the tactical use of all weapons, nor are they able to lead the units independently using the technology available effectively. As a result, a group of senior armed forces officials was sent for one-year training to the Union of Soviet Socialist Republics. Upon their return, the command is to be reorganised to meet the requirements of the modern army. A number of command cadres were also sent to schools in the Czechoslovak Socialist Republic to ensure that the new system is gradually brought to life when the country's armed forces decided to introduce a system that is being implemented in socialist countries.[32]

COLONEL'S VISIT TO CZECHOSLOVAKIA

Bilateral relations between Tripoli and Prague culminated in 1978 when the Czechoslovak capital was visited by Libyan leader Muammar Gaddafi. His large delegation arrived in Prague on 20 June and stayed there for three days. The communist state propaganda machinery went into overdrive and claimed that Gaddafi is one of the 'progressively oriented representatives of the Arab world who strongly oppose imperialist interference in the affairs of the Arab countries and the whole of Africa. On his initiative, Libya is constantly expanding friendly relations with socialist countries, including Czechoslovakia'. In order to enhance the prospects of sales of additional Czechoslovak weapons to Libya, President Gustáv Husák awarded Gaddafi the highest Czechoslovak state award – the Order of the White Lion Class I with collar 'for merits in the development of mutual Czechoslovak-Libyan relations and successful cooperation'. In his speech, Husák called Gaddafi 'the great son of the Libyan people who stood at the forefront of the revolutionary transformations of Libyan society, as well as the great son of the Arab people who are at the forefront

A MiG-23UB of the Libyan Arab Air Force seen at Mitiga Airbase in 1976. The Czechoslovak military representatives in the country seem to have entirely missed a major drama that developed during the late 1970s, when as a result of a series of fatal accidents with this type, the Libyans ceased sending their personnel to the USSR for training, and hired two veteran US fighter-pilots to test-fly and write them a new manual for the type. (Albert Grandolini collection)

of the efforts of the Arab progressive forces for their freedom and independence'.

As usual, the shipments of arms and military assistance were on the top of the agenda. The respective negotiations took place on 21 and 22 June 1978 and included the checking of the implementation of the Protocol from 17 May 1977, where 'both parties stated that most of the commitments were being successfully implemented'. The bulk of the deliveries according to the Protocol (80 vz. 70 GRAD multiple rocket launchers, 72 L-39ZO Albatros jet trainers, and 350 vehicles of the T-55 series) was on schedule.

Libyan representatives led by Colonel Muftah F Dakhil, Chief of the Directorate of Military Procurement of the Libyan Arab Armed Forces, submitted new requirements for arms supplies:

- 7,000 vz. 58 assault rifles,
- 15,000 hand grenades,
- 10,000 anti-personnel mines,
- 5,000 anti-tank mines,
- 2,000 RPG-75 single-shot anti-tank weapons,
- 500 RPG-Cv-75 training weapons,
- 144 9S415 control units for 9K11 Malyutka,
- 4,320 9M14M anti-tank guided missiles for 9K11 Malyutka,
- 500,000 vz. 43 7.62mm ammunition.

At the same time, the Libyan delegation expressed interest in the delivery of 200 BVP-1 infantry fighting vehicles, brand new vz. 77 DANA self-propelled gun howitzers, and L-410 transport aircraft.

During negotiations with Husák, Gaddafi expanded the original requirement for 200 BVP-1s to 600 vehicles.

An important point in the negotiations was Libya's repeated request for cooperation in the establishment of a local military industry. Specifically, Libyan officials were interested in construction of plants for the manufacturing of Aero L-39 Albatros training aircraft, vz. 70 GRAD multiple rocket launchers, T-55 tanks, and 9M14M Malyutka anti-tank guided missiles. Prague responded to Libyan demands in February 1979 during bilateral negotiations in Libya. HTS boss František Langer announced there that Czechoslovakia did not have authorisation to introduce the production of Soviet tanks and anti-tank guided missiles. However, he expressed the willingness to negotiate projects for a plant for the production of L-39 and L-410 aircraft, a plant for the production of the weapon superstructures for the vz. 70 multiple rocket launchers, a plant for the production of spare parts for T-55 tanks, and a plant for the production of large-calibre ammunition.

Moreover, Langer confirmed the Czechoslovak readiness to build a plant for the production of infantry weapons and ammunition according to the Protocol from 17 May 1977. Following the Libyan request, Czechoslovakia prepared a project study of this facility that was approved by the Libyan authorities in November 1978.

However, Czechoslovak representatives were fully aware of the unrealistic nature of Libyan demands since Libya had 'no raw materials, materials, skilled labour, experience and even the production of these special materials in the Czechoslovak Socialist Republic is largely (e.g. for L-39 up to 60 % of the content) dependent on imports'.[33]

A Soviet-manufactured BMP-1 infantry fighting vehicle of the Libyan Arab Army seen in a parade in Tripoli during 1978. The Czechoslovak licensed variant – the BVP-1 – was supplied to Libya from 1980 onward. Notable are the hull number applied on top of the lower glacis plate, and an 9M14 Malyutka (ASCC/NATO reporting name 'AT-3 Sagger') anti-tank missile installed on its launcher, atop the vehicle's gun. (Tom Cooper collection)

Muammar Gaddafi arriving at Ruzyně International Airport for an official visit to Czechoslovakia in 1978. (via Martin Smisek)

Gaddafi seen with Gustáv Husák – the First Secretary of the Communist Party of Czechoslovakia, and vice-premier from 1968 to 1975 (before assuming the position of the President of Czechoslovakia, from 1975 to 1989) – at Prague Castle, when the latter decorated him with the White Lion 1st Class medal. (via Martin Smisek)

THE ALBATROS FOR THE LIBYAN ARAB AIR FORCE

Colonel Gaddafi was not only an honoured client of Czechoslovak-made T-55 tanks but also a solvent customer for L-39ZO Albatros training and light combat aircraft. Indeed, Libya became the second-largest operator of L-39 trainers after the Soviet Union. Negotiations for the delivery of the first L-39 airplanes began in 1976. The following year, representatives of OMNIPOL and the Libyan Ministry of Defence signed the relevant agreement for the acquisition of 72 L-39ZOs. The first 36 aircraft were acquired by the Libyan Arab Air Force (LAAF) during the summer and autumn of 1978.

The planes were flown to Libya by Czechoslovak civilian aircrews and had Czechoslovak civil aircraft registrations for the purposes of the flight. The HTS originally assumed that the flights would be performed by military pilots, as was the case with the delivery of the L-39 to Afghanistan because the production plant did not have enough of its own pilots. In a letter dated 26 October 1977, Minister of Foreign Trade Andrej Barčák turned to Minister of National Defence Army General Martin Dzúr with a request to provide crews for the flights of Albatros trainers to Libya. However, the answer was negative. Military pilots did not have a civilian pilot's license and were not prepared to fly in conditions of civil international air traffic, where English was used for communication (delivery flights to Afghanistan were carried out through the Soviet Union with the full support of the Soviet Air Force which did not require Czechoslovak military pilots to have civilian aviation diplomas). The HTS had to find another solution. Therefore, the pilots and navigators of Czechoslovak Airlines were involved in the flights to Libya.

During the delivery of the first 36 L-39ZOs, one aircraft was destroyed in a crash near Brno-Tuřany airport. The reason was the indiscipline during the flight from the factory airport in Vodochody to Libya. Pilot František Horčičko had flown L-39 jet trainers to foreign customers several times before and he was the only one who often made low passes over the airports, sometimes even with a roll. His actions were tolerated by others, but on 29 September 1978, they became fatal for him and his navigator Hrubý. That day he had drop tanks on his L-39ZO, their luggage was in the cockpit, and during the roll, for unknown reasons, he reduced throttle. Subsequently, he lost control of his airplane and it crashed, both crew members, originally aircrew of Czechoslovak Airlines, were killed.

Additional L-39ZOs were supplied in 1979, 1981, 1982, and 1983. In total, the Libyan Arab Air Force became the user of 180 Albatros trainers. Together with the aircraft, four TL-39 flight simulators and two NKTL-29/39 ejection simulators were delivered between 1979 and 1980. The aircraft were initially introduced into the inventory of the 1st Training Wing at Okba ben Nafi airbase (formerly Wheelus Field, in western Libya) and the 2nd Training Wing at Ghurdabiya air base, south of Syrte. To support their operation and training of new Libyan pilots, a large contingent of Czechoslovak Air Force instructors and advisors was dispatched to Libya in the late 1970s under the codename Operation Litomyšl. The Czechoslovak advisory group remained in Libya until the end of the next decade. Up to then, there had been more than 30 serious accidents in which at least six pilots had died.

For the elementary training, Libyans used Italian SIAI-Marchetti SF.260 piston training aircraft. The syllabus then continued with training flights on Czechoslovak L-39ZOs or Yugoslav G-2As. In addition to Libyan pilots, the L-39ZOs of the Libyan Arab Air Force were used for the training of new military fliers from Algeria, Ghana, and Niger. Later, the aircraft were equipped with UB-16-

57 rocket pods, each for 16 S-5 57mm unguided rockets, and used for border patrols. Besides this, the armed Albatros aircraft were deployed during Gaddafi's military adventures in Chad between 1983 to 1987. During the final Chadian offensive in March 1987, the Chadians captured Wadi Doum airfield along with 10 L-39ZOs. Two additional Albatros airplanes of the Libyan Arab Air Force were shot down by ground fire in the course of the fighting.[34]

Table 23: Overview of L-39 Albatros training aircraft delivered to Libya, 1978–1989[35]

Year	Variant	Number of examples	Hand over, overflight
1978	L-39ZO.1	36 (35)	9 June 1978 – 29 September 1978, one aircraft crashed on 29 September 1978 during the flight to Libya
1979	L-39ZO.1	37	25 May 1979 – 21 September 1979
1981	L-39ZO.1	8	19 May 1981 – 2 June 1981
1981	L-39ZO.1	13	20 October 1981 – 17 November 1981
1982	L-39ZO.1	8	27 May 1982 – 8 June 1982
1982	L-39ZO.1	36	22 June 1982 – 12 October 1982
1983	L-39ZO.1	26	29 March 1983 – 21 June 1983
1983	L-39ZO.1	17	21 June 1983 – 19 July 1983

A pre-delivery photograph of an Aero L-39ZO Albatros training jet manufactured for Libya. Notable is the application of the crest of the Libyan Arab Air Force Academy below the front portion of the cockpit. (Tom Cooper collection)

PREPARATIONS FOR LIBYAN DEPLOYMENT

During negotiations on the supply of Czechoslovak weapons, Tripoli conditioned their purchase by sending a huge number of Czechoslovak military personnel to Libya, where it would provide appropriate training to local troops. Since the arms deals with the Libyans were immensely lucrative, the communist leadership in Prague decided to accept Libyan demands and in the Protocol of 17 May 1977 undertook to provide long-term military assistance by sending several hundred Czechoslovak instructors and advisors to Libya, although this created an extreme strain in the Czechoslovak People's Army. The undertaking was approved by the Czechoslovak government in Resolution No. 136 on 16 June 1977 and received the Czechoslovak cover name Operation Litomyšl (Litomyšl is a town which lies 136 kilometres [85 miles] east of Prague), which was also known in the shortened form simply as Operation L. It represented the largest continuous deployment of Czechoslovak soldiers abroad during the whole Cold War. Due to the immense scope of the operation, Czechoslovakia deployed to Libya not only career soldiers and civilian employees of the Federal Ministry of National Defence but also a large number of draft soldiers and even reservists.[36]

In August 1977, a huge recruitment campaign began in the Czechoslovak People's Army. While career officers and non-commissioned officers were being selected for the position of teacher, the draft soldiers were being selected into the role of instructors. First, recruiters selected future instructors from the ranks of soldiers who had almost completed their two-year military service and were to return to civilian life in the fall of 1977. Contrary to the original expectations, however, the required numbers from this age category were far from being met. The selection was made according to certain preconditions, for example, how a soldier was punished during his military compulsory service. Moreover, not everyone was interested in participating in this adventure. And so it happened that the recruiters were forced to offer this job to soldiers who were just in their first year of military service. The paradox was that often professionally inexperienced first-year troops served the second year of their duty for lucrative financial conditions as instructors abroad.

Beginning on 12 September 1977, selected specialists earmarked for deployment in Libya underwent preparatory professional, medical, and language training at three training centres. Additional communist indoctrination was also a part of it. On 12 and 13 October, a special committee from the Combat Training Directorate (*Správa bojové přípravy*) from the General Staff of the Czechoslovak People's Army carried out an inspection at the garrisons of Kežmarok and Brezno to verify the state of preparedness of members of the various training teams designated for deployment in Libya. Overall, the achieved level was evaluated as good, although sometimes problems with the discipline were present:

> It was managed to eliminate some negative phenomena also in Kežmarok garrison, especially excessive alcohol consumption, violation of the principles of socialist morality in the contact of experts with the civilian public, etc. The elimination of these shortcomings positively helped the public hearing of the cases of comrade Minář, a member of the Communist Party of Czechoslovakia, who attacked the guard in a drunken state and behaved rudely and defiantly during the commander's investigation of this case.

Every member of the Czechoslovak military training contingent underwent a short-term language course in English. However, due to the different motivations and talent, the results were mixed:

> The results of studying English in the Brezno group are very different due to the shortness of the course. In addition to barely 10 % of excellent students who have the prerequisites for further successful growth, most show poor to insufficient results, mainly due to lack of interest in learning English.

Based on General Contract No. 4575 (Supplements No. 1 to No. 7) concluded by the HTS, three groups of Czechoslovak ground

forces advisors were prepared for deployment to Libya. These were intended for:

- tank training: 84 crews for T-55 tanks (336 instructors), 12 crews for VT-55 armoured recovery vehicles (36 instructors), 36 command and technical experts, 24 interpreters, and 3 doctors;
- artillery training: six crews for vz. 70 multiple rocket launchers (24 instructors), two crews for M-46 guns (18 instructors), and 44 artillery specialists including interpreters;
- repairs and storage of tanks, multiple rocket launchers, and armoured personnel carriers: 35 technical experts.

At the end of October 1977, 556 experts were ready for deployment to Libya, of which 449 were conscripts, 90 career soldiers, three reserve soldiers, and 14 civilian employees. The transfer of all members was carried out by eight Czechoslovak Airlines Il-18 aircraft to Tripoli and Benghazi airports from 28 October to 3 November 1977 (for details see Table 24). However, in the end, 555 Czechoslovak advisors were transported to Libya since one tank driver ended up in medical treatment at the Military Hospital Košice (*Vojenská nemocnice Košice*). He was transported to Libya later in November.

Besides, according to General Contract No. 4575 (Supplement No. 8), 44 Czechoslovak aviation specialists were to provide training for Libyan pilots and technicians on L-39ZO Albatros aircraft in the school year 1977/1978. The first five advisors from this group had been working in Libya since 28 September 1977. The remaining 39 instructors were concentrated in the air base in Piešťany, where their political, professional, language, and medical training took place from 18 October 1977. They were transported to Libya in early December 1977.

The activities of all Czechoslovak military advisors deployed to Libya were coordinated by a nine-member command and control team under the command of Major General Juraj Lalo. Its initial section composed of four officers began operating in Libya on 21 October 1977. Major General Lalo flew from Czechoslovakia on 28 November. The remaining members of his team arrived in Libya on 2 November.[37]

A Czechoslovak Air Force instructor with his Libyan students. (Václav Havner collection)

Table 24: Deployment of the first rotation of Czechoslovak ground forces advisors to Libya, 1977[38]

Departure from Czechoslovakia	General Contract No. 4575	Specialisation	Number of Advisors	Planned General Area Of Deployment	Aircraft of Czechoslovak Airlines
28 October	Supplement No. 6	repairmen of vz. 70 multiple rocket launchers	7	Tripoli	Il-18V OK-PAE, Il-18V OK-PAG, Il-18V OK-PAH (transported 223 persons)
	Supplement No. 2	T-55 tank crews	145	Tripoli	
	Supplement No. 2	T-55 tank crews	73	Tobruk	
29 October	Supplement No. 2	T-55 tank crews	72	Tobruk	Il-18V OK-PAE (transported 79 persons)
	Supplement No. 4	team leaders for repairs of T-55 tanks	6	Tobruk	
30 October	Supplement No. 2	T-55 tank crews	73	Benghazi	Il-18V OK-PAG (transported 72 persons)
31 October	Supplement No. 2	T-55 tank crews	72	Benghazi	Il-18V OK-PAE (transported 72 persons)
2 November	Supplement No. 1	vz. 70 multiple rocket launcher crews	37	Tripoli	Il-18V OK-PAE (transported 54 persons)
	Supplement No. 5	advisors repairs of T-55 tanks	3	Tripoli	
	Supplement No. 3	experts on storage of T-55 spare parts	13	Tripoli	
3 November	Supplement No. 7	crews for M-46 guns	49	Tripoli	Il-18E OK-PAI (transported 55 persons)
	Supplement No. 4	team leaders for repairs of T-55 tanks	6	Tripoli	

OPERATION LITOMYŠL BEGINS

From 30 October to 1 November, Major General Juraj Lalo held several negotiations with his Libyan counterparts, aiming to clarify the exact areas of deployment for the individual Czechoslovak tank and artillery advisory teams.

Upon the arrival of the first Czechoslovak advisors, it turned out that their accommodation was not sufficiently prepared by the Libyan side. Only in the morning did the Libyans manage to secure accommodation in various hotels for them. Two teams of 72 Czechoslovak tank experts deployed at Tobruk were accommodated on the premises of a local tank repair workshop. The members of the command and control group were temporarily housed in the Czechoslovak embassy in Tripoli which also served as their headquarters. Later, the staff of the command and control group worked and lived at a 12-story apartment building rented from the company African Trade and Import Co Ltd in Tripoli.

At the request of the leadership of the Libyan Arab Armed Forces, Czechoslovak personnel trained troops of the Libyan Arab Army in three areas: Tripoli, Benghazi, and Tobruk. Directly in Tripoli or its immediate vicinity operated a command and control group (nine persons), instructors for training on vz. 70 multiple rocket launchers and M-46 guns (86 persons), and experts for storage, tank repairs, and repairs of vz. 70 multiple rocket launchers (29 persons). The Czechoslovak advisors (145 persons) for the training of Libyan T-55 tank crews served in the areas of Tripoli, Sabratha (70 kilometres [47 miles] west of Tripoli), and Sirte (375 kilometres [233 miles] southeast of Tripoli). In the Benghazi area, there were four tank training teams with a total of 145 persons. One of these four teams composed of 36 men was deployed in Marj (100 kilometres [62 miles] east of Benghazi). Another 145 Czechoslovak instructors trained Libyan tank crews with two teams in Bomba (100 kilometres [62 miles] west of Tobruk) and two teams in Tobruk. Besides, six tank repair specialists expanded the Czechoslovak advisory team at Workshop No. 3 at Tobruk, which had been operating there since April 1977.

The work of the Czechoslovak military training contingent in their respective areas commenced on 1 November at Tobruk, on 3 November at Benghazi, and around 10 November at Tripoli. The very first activities of the Czechoslovak personnel focused mainly on maintenance, ensuring operability, and storage of supplied military hardware and spare parts. The first experience confirmed the assumption that the main difficulties would lie in the lack of knowledge of the English language in the units of the Libyan Arab Army, which would be trained by the Czechoslovak instructors.[39]

In his memo from 15 December 1977, Chief of the General Staff of the Czechoslovak People's Army Colonel General Karel Rusov warned the commander of the Czechoslovak military training contingent in Libya Major General Juraj Lalo as follows:

I would like to draw your attention to the efforts of the Libyan authorities to provoke in conversations with Czechoslovak experts disputes between them and experts from other socialist states by emphasising the benefits and a more responsible attitude to the fulfilment of tasks by experts from other socialist countries. Therefore, ensure the complete restraint of Czechoslovak experts in talks with Libyans about the tasks and approach to their fulfilment by experts from other socialist countries.

Although the Czechoslovak Ambassador Varholík strictly prohibited the military advisors from use hitchhiking during their leisure time because of 'the danger of using hitchhiking in local conditions', his words fell on barren ground. Thus, the first casualties of the Czechoslovak military training contingent in Libya were caused for this very reason. On 2 December 1977 at 10:00 a.m., a car accident occurred in Tripoli, in which Jasoň Pivec died and Jan Celba was seriously injured. Both interpreters used hitchhiking despite the ban issued. The car was driven by Palestinian doctor Mohamed Atifa who crashed his Toyota into a tree by the road while driving too fast. Atifa was also seriously wounded. The Minister of National Defence, the ÚV KSČ general secretary, and the President in Prague were informed about the incident.

Jan Celba was operated on in Tripoli hospital by the Bulgarian neurosurgeon Pacov. Despite all the care given, he remained unconscious and his life was in danger. Since his condition did not improve, Lieutenant Colonel Dr. Ivo Fusek from the neurosurgical department of the Central Military Hospital Prague (*Ústřední vojenská nemocnice Praha*) arrived in Tripoli and remained there until 21 December. According to a report which arrived in Prague on 29 December, Jan Celba's health began to deteriorate. Therefore, Lieutenant Colonel. Dr. Ivo Fusek flew to Tripoli the next day and performed the necessary surgery immediately upon his arrival. Because conditions in Libya did not provide the necessary postoperative medical and nursing regime, Jan Celba was transported to the Central Military Hospital Prague on 4 January 1978. Despite all the specialised care, the condition of the wounded remained very serious. This had not been reversed even with the use of the most modern drugs available. Jan Celba succumbed to his serious injuries on 5 February 1978.[40]

THE INSTRUCTOR AT ROCKET LAUNCHERS

One of the more than 580 Czechoslovak military instructors and advisors deployed in late 1977 in Libya was the driver of vz. 70 GRAD multiple rocket launcher Václav Háva. His two-year compulsory military service was slowly reaching its end when he was presented with a financially very lucrative offer in August 1977 – to become a military instructor in an Arab country. According to the terms of the contract, the advisory team, of which he was a member, was tasked with training one Libyan rocket launcher battalion within one year. Václav Háva remembered his subsequent service in the Socialist People's Libyan Arab Jamahiriya as follows:

I completed a two-month preparatory course. One cold and bleak November day, the weathered Il-18 detached itself from Ruzyně airport and headed for Libya. The whole group numbered about twenty men. When boarding this plane, everyone was worried about whether the aircraft would stay in the air for the next several thousand kilometres at all because shortly before that, a plane of the same type crashed near Bratislava. After a few hours of flight, however, surprisingly, the landing area of the airport in the capital of Libya, Tripoli, appeared below us and we managed to land successfully there.

[…]

A Libyan officer with a Colt at his waist was already waiting for us in the airport lobby, which surprised us very much. And as it turned out later, it was not for the first time, many more surprises awaited us later.

[…]

At the beginning of December, the training started in full swing. Rocket launchers and other equipment travelled from Czechoslovakia by train to Yugoslavia and then by Czechoslovak ship to the port of Tripoli. We assisted in unloading the equipment from the ship to prevent any damage. Our ship was moored at the pier, which was intended for military purposes, so we could see many very interesting things for ourselves. A Soviet ship was moored nearby, and huge cranes were pulling elongated, narrow crates from inside it.

[…]

The instruction itself took place five days a week, from Sunday to Thursday, Friday was a day when all the students concentrated on the central parade ground of the camp and the clergyman read excerpts from the Koran to them. We were not idle either, we sat in the classroom and discussed Marx-Leninist preparation. The leader of our group always appointed one of us to read various political articles from the two-week-old Rudé právo newspaper.

[…]

Saturday was a day off, so we spent this time exploring not only the capital but also historically interesting monuments from the time when Libya was inhabited by the Romans. We loved Leptis Magna and Sabrata, the ancient coastal cities, so much that we visited them several times during our stay.

[…]

Teaching Libyan students to master the military hardware was not as easy as it initially seemed. The topic first had to be interpreted from Czech into English, which was provided by a Czech interpreter. Then from English to Arabic, this role was taken over by an Arabic interpreter, and it was very lengthy. Another problem was that Libyan Arabic has a very small vocabulary and some Czech terms simply do not exist in Arabic. For example, the rocket launcher is based on the chassis of the Tatra 813, the truck has a relatively complex transmission, part of which is, among other things, the so-called planetary overdrive, and that was a tough nut to crack for interpreters. According to the curriculum, I had two hours on this topic, but it was far from enough. There has been much arguing about how to translate this term. No wonder one of the students fell asleep with boredom on the desk. Therefore, I warned the sergeant in charge of the class to wake the concerned student. I later regretted this order because followed something that we were not used to in our army. The sergeant woke the soldier, but immediately after the next recess he literally pulled him to an obstacle course, where he ordered him to do squats in the moat first and later push-ups. The student made a hero of himself, he pleaded with the sergeant, and so the worst happened. The sergeant broke a branch from a nearby tree, with which he properly beat the student in such a way that his friends had to take him to the infirmary where he was recovering for a week. It was incomprehensible to us that the whole incident was watched from the distance by the camp commander with satisfaction and a smile on the lips. We later learned that the sergeant in question had even received praise for strengthening morale.

Another handicap for us was the fact that some students were much older than us, which is why Libyan officers did not trust us at first. They thought that, given our age, we might not even have the experience to teach. Some escalation occurred after we moved from theory to actual field training.

There are time norms for all activities around the rocket launcher that Libyan students did not catch up with. At that time, the camp commander was Captain Barany. […] He visited the chief of our group and explained to him the opinion of subordinate commanders who thought that the time norms were unrealistic and that they could not be met in any case. It has gone so far that he suggested that even the instructors themselves would not meet these standards. Finally, he asked whether Czechoslovak instructors could demonstrate assuming the firing position in the prescribed standards. The Libyans were distrustful of us. By no means did he want to admit that we wouldn't be able to put together complete crews. Professional pride and honour told us to do everything we could to prove that we were in our places. After proper preparation, a demonstration took place which, except for small shortcomings nonvisible to the Libyans, succeeded. We probably rose in price, the words of appreciation followed through interpreters.

Once the practice rides began, first off-road and later on the road, all communication between the instructor and the student was in Arabic and without an interpreter. Therefore, we had no choice but to learn at least the basic phrases. In the end, we adopted the local customs. If a student incorrectly engaged a gear while driving, each instructor had a beech wood gauge at hand, which was commonly used to measure the amount of fuel in the tank. In this case, however, it was used as a "negotiation tool", surprisingly, this method was very effective.

[…]

[Around the second week of September 1978], the entire rocket launcher battalion underwent a live firing exercise. Everything went smoothly until the commanders of the individual crews, after aiming the rocket launcher at the target and receiving the order to fire, became so afraid that the firing key in question was eventually turned by the instructor himself. The rocket launcher swayed under the onslaught of departing rockets, huge clouds of swirling sand around, and after a few seconds, it was all over. The entire frightened Libyan crew breathed a sigh of relief.

Before returning to the homeland, the entire rocket launcher battalion received an order to move. The destination was an oasis about a thousand kilometres [(621 miles)] south in the desert called Sebha. We thought that this move did not concern us, but everything was different. The Libyans were worried about possible defects of the equipment, so we also had to participate in this anabasis as a technical accompaniment. The whole trip lasted several days, after about every 200 kilometres [(124 miles)] we replenished water and fuel in the oases. By no means was it a walk through the rose garden, once it even happened to us that in one oasis, after pumping water and driving a few kilometres, we found small worms swimming. As a result, this liquid was for drinking unusable, a rather big problem in the given situation.[41]

Beyond expectations, despite language and often organisational problems, the entire training can be assessed as continuous, and so it happened that we managed to train rocket launcher crews half a year earlier than planned. Based on the negotiations, the contract was extended because we had signed employment contracts for one year.

The command group decided that we would train another rocket launcher battalion. Of course, there was also some financial compensation. The year passes just like water in a river and the whole group was preparing to return to the homeland. Some were offered an extension of their employment contract. A few individuals, perhaps out of a desire for greater financial gain, accepted the offer. However, this chance did not appeal to most of them, after a year of separation from their families, everyone was looking forward to going home.[42]

HUSÁK'S *AFRIKAKORPS*

At the beginning of Operation Litomyšl, the main emphasis was placed on the training of Libyan tank crews according to Supplement No. 2 of General Contract No. 4575. This task was performed by a total of 10 training teams with cover names A-1 to C-10 in the areas of Tripoli, Benghazi, and Tobruk, as detailed in Table 25.[43]

Table 25: Czechoslovak tank training teams in Libya, November 1977[44]

Cover designation	Specialisation	Number of advisors	Area of deployment
A-1	training of T-55 tank crews	36	Tobruk
A-2	training of T-55 tank crews	36	Tobruk
A-3	training of T-55 tank crews	36	Bomba
A-4	training of T-55 tank crews	36	Bomba
B-5	training of T-55 tank crews	37	Benghazi
B-6	training of T-55 tank crews	36	Benghazi
B-7	training of T-55 tank crews	36	Benghazi
B-8	training of T-55 tank crews	36	Marj
C-9	training of T-55 tank crews	37	Tripoli
C-10	training of T-55 tank crews	36	Tajura

This mission was completed in 1978 and the Libyans did not demand further training of T-55 tank crews in the forthcoming years. As a result, on 31 October 1978 up to 380 Czechoslovak instructors ceased operations on behalf of the Libyan Arab Armed Forces. At that time, 792 Czechoslovak military experts were working in Libya, of which 520 performed tank and artillery training. Nevertheless, in 1979, 13 Czechoslovak tank training teams were deployed in Libya, numbering 115 persons. Their activities were mainly focused on repairs and maintenance of tanks and armoured personnel carriers, storage of equipment, and building of training facilities.

Compared to the previous year, there was a better fulfilment of tasks, which resulted from the experience gained from the first year of activity. Nevertheless, it was not possible to ensure the full use of all Czechoslovak advisors and instructors in all localities who very often had to perform replacement work. The main reason was the lack of Libyan interpreters for translations from English into Arabic. One of the most important tasks of Czechoslovak advisors in 1979 was the preparation of Libyan armoured vehicles for a military parade commemorating the 10th anniversary of the revolution. During the year, individual teams, originally contracted for the training of troops, worked on building training facilities, technical preparation of armoured vehicles for training, as well as repairs and maintenance of tanks and armoured personnel carriers.

In 1979, four groups with a total of 62 Czechoslovak artillery specialists worked in Libya. Two teams trained Libyans on vz. 70 GRAD multiple rocket launchers, one team trained M-46 gun crews. The last group instructed Libyan technical personnel on the maintenance and repairs of vz. 70 multiple rocket launchers. The results in the training of Libyan commanders, non-commissioned officers, and soldiers were rated as very good.

During the year, a number of cooperative exercises of the Libyan Arab Army with the live shooting of units armed with vz. 70 multiple rocket launchers and M-46 guns, where Czechoslovak advisors worked, took place. The most extensive ones were undertaken on 25 April, 18 June, and 10 October. The results of shooting not only in these exercises but also during individual exercises of respective artillery and rocket launcher battalions were consistently very good.

The results of the advisory and training activity of the Czechoslovak artillery experts in 1979 were summarised in an internal report as follows:

The participation and results achieved in the exercises of the artillery battalions confirmed the high degree of proficiency of all specialisations capable of performing combat tasks independently, accurately, in time, and in cooperation with other arms. Also vz. 70 122mm rocket launchers made in Czechoslovakia proved their qualities in difficult conditions when moving long distances day and night and using all their combat capabilities to conduct accurate and effective fire.

The excellent evaluation of artillery units by the highest political and military representatives of Libya is also the best assessment of the work of Czechoslovak military experts in the artillery specialisation. However, the results required great efforts from Czechoslovak military experts to promote the principles of proper combat use of artillery armament, safety measures in shooting, and proper administration of combat documentation because the Libyan commanders underestimated these issues. Also, the high consumption of ammunition to achieve a visual and sound effect did not comply with the principles of the rules of shooting and the technical capabilities of artillery materiel. Only after consultations of the workers of the command group with the commanders of the first party, the recommendations of Czechoslovak military experts were fully respected.

As of 1 December 1979, there were 540 Czechoslovak air force and ground forces advisors together with 179 wives and 170 children in Libya. Libyan demands for the presence of Czechoslovak ground forces instructors gradually declined, so the assistance of only eight tank and three artillery teams was contracted for the year 1980 (for details, see Table 26). This downward trend continued in the following years. On the other hand, the training activities of Czechoslovak Air Force personnel in Libya had a constantly growing tendency.[45]

Table 26: Czechoslovak ground forces advisory groups in Libya, 1980[46]

Number of the group	Cover designation	Specialization	Number of advisors	Area of deployment
1	H	maintenance and storage of tanks	3	Tajura
2	B-6	maintenance and preservation of armoured personnel carriers	27	Tajura
3	C-12	maintenance and preservation of tanks	28	Tajura
4	G	repairs of tanks and armoured personnel carriers	7	Tajura
5	J	storage of tank equipment	33	Tajura
6	Sirte	repairs of tanks	25	Sirte
7	F	repairs of tanks and armoured personnel carriers	13	Benghazi
8	T	medium overhauls of tanks	15	Tobruk
9	D-1	training on vz. 70 multiple rocket launchers	15	Sirte
10	D-2	training on vz. 70 multiple rocket launchers	7	Sebha
11	E	training on M-46 guns	7	Sirte

ASSISTANCE FOR THE LIBYAN ARAB AIR FORCE

Within the frame of Resolution No. 136 from 16 June 1977, the Czechoslovak government ordered the Czechoslovak Air Force to establish the Secondary Aviation School (for the training of pilots and technical personnel) in Libya and to train Libyan aircrews (pilots and navigators) in the Czechoslovak Socialist Republic.

The advisory mission of the Czechoslovak Air Force personnel – instructor pilots, aircraft technicians, and other supporting ground crews – began in earnest in 1977 when 44 instructors arrived in Tripoli in September and December to fulfil the terms of Supplement No 8 of the General Contract No. 4575. Since September 1977, the first Czechoslovak advisors provided theoretical education, practical flight training commenced in December 1978.[47]

The work of the Czechoslovak Air Force advisory group concentrated on the training in the Secondary Aviation School at Tripoli that was officially established on 1 September 1978, the 9th anniversary of Gaddafi's coup. During the opening ceremonial air show, Czechoslovak military pilots demonstrated brand new L-39ZO Albatros training and light combat aircraft which required the direct consent of Minister of National Defence Army General Martin Dzúr.

In 1979, 1,122 Libyan cadets were trained, of which 253 were in flight training. Practical flight training was started with 129 cadets, of which 120 performed the first solo flights. In the school year 1979/1980, which began on 17 October 1979, three grades of cadets were in training, numbering a total of 1,311 students (the first grade 400 cadets, the second grade 398 cadets, the third grade 513 cadets). Theoretical teaching was planned and led by a team of Czechoslovak advisors in cooperation with the deputy commander of the Secondary Aviation School, Major Saleh.

However, the training of Libyan cadets did not go without problems: 'The effectiveness of teaching cadets is not proportional to the efforts of teachers due to the low basic general knowledge of cadets and knowledge of the English language'.

For the execution of flight training, the Secondary Aviation School had in its structure the 1st Training Wing which was deployed at Okba ben Nafi AB. The wing later had four squadrons of 10 instructor pilots, each of whom usually trained three cadets. The wing and individual squadrons were led by Czechoslovak commanders who were responsible for the actual flight training. In 1978, they were Lieutenant Colonel Dokoupil (wing commander), Major Petřík, Lieutenant Colonel Ľachký, Major Vyhnálek, and Lieutenant Colonel Jaroš (squadron commanders). The positions were doubled by Libyan officers who took care of all other matters, including disciplinary practice which was sometimes quite harsh, at least according to the standards of the Czechoslovak People's Army.

The sluggishness of Libyan officials caused the delayed start of various phases of training. For this reason, flight training with Libyan cadets on L-39ZO aircraft did not start until 24 December 1978.

In June 1979, there was an aircraft accident involving an L-39ZO trainer, in which the instructor pilot Major Zdeněk Hájek and the cadet Habib died. By 1 December 1979, a total of 8,902 flight hours had been flown during 29,169 flights. This high tempo was ensured through careful maintenance and repairs of Albatros trainers by Czechoslovak technicians. Despite considerable language problems for both cadets and Czechoslovak instructor pilots, the basic stage of training was completed by 120 Libyans who made their first solo flights during 1979. Nine cadets were expelled from further training at the end of August 1979 due to health problems or the inability to learn to fly. Another seven cadets were dismissed for their inability to continue in solo flying and due to their failure to pass the second-year exams. Besides, on 1 November 1979, two TL-39 simulators were put into operation on which the training of Libyan student pilots immediately began.

In addition to theoretical education and flight training, the Czechoslovak aviation advisory team prepared associated classrooms, laboratories, and workshops. A number of necessary textbooks, illustrative teaching aids, and translations were prepared to ensure proper teaching and training. During the flight training, four Libyan officers underwent a conversion course on the L-39ZO: the wing commander and the squadron commanders. In 1979, Czechoslovak instructor pilots participated in three parades, where they demonstrated acrobatics with the Albatros aircraft.

To increase the capacity of flight training undertaken by the Secondary Aviation School, the 2nd Training Wing was established at Okba ben Nafi air base on 1 December 1979. Part of the unit was initially moved to al-Woutiya AB, lying some 150 kilometres (93 miles) west of Tripoli. However, in early February 1980, the unit was completely redeployed to Ghurdabiya AB, some 360 kilometres (224 miles) southeast of Tripoli, and began operations with the flight training of 124 Libyan cadets.

The activities of the Czechoslovak aviation advisory group in Libya were complicated by shortcomings on both the Libyan and Czechoslovak sides:

Due to the inconsistency of the Libyan side in adhering to the plan, there were frequent changes in teaching during the year, which disrupted the methodology and quality of teaching, especially in the first grade.

Weaknesses in the material support of teaching and training are related to the low activity business of our trade organisations on Libyan demand. Defects of aircraft, non-compliance with contracted agreements, and poor quality supplies of support equipment and laboratory and workshop equipment damage the good name of the Czechoslovak Socialist Republic and the efforts of our experts in technical assistance. Failure to address some major issues, such as general overhauls of aircraft and engines, which the Libyan side has been asking about for over a year, does not indicate the thoroughness and seriousness of our foreign trade here in Libya.[48]

A total of 618 Czechoslovak aviation specialists were contracted for the theoretical teaching and flight training for the years 1979 to 1981: 86 pilots, 412 ground crews for support of flying operations, and 120 theory teachers and interpreters.[49]

GROUP

GARIAN

	1st SQUADRON				3th SQUADRON		
In.	CADET	Call s.	Mil.no.	Instr.	CADET	Call s.	Mil.no.
LICHT. 010				MARTE. 020			
ŠUFL. 011				SMÉK. 021			
ORYGAR 012	HASSAN	030	2815	NOVOTNÝ 022	HARARI	062	2879
	HARON	031	3179		MARIM	063	3402
	SALEM	032	S-73		IBRAHIM	064	S-67
MAKZUM 013	SALMA	033	3411	ADNAN 023	AZAM	065	3099
	RAMADAN	034	2856		LUTFI	066	3141
	SALAH	035	2037		ADAM	067	2794
MARAI 014	ABDELSALAM	036	2977	EL TUMI 024	SOLA	068	2898
	AMAR	037	2983		RAMADAN	069	2077
	ABDELHAFED	038	2991		ZOHRA	070	3403
BSSATED 015	ALADEL	039	2985	ALI MOHAM. 025	MUFTAH	071	3157
	BASHER	040	3000		SHUKRI	072	2916
	AHMED	041	S-70		AGILA	073	2809
HŘEBAČKA 016	SUAD	042	3422	FIŠER 026	SLIM	074	2909
	OMRAN	043	3024		SHARIF	075	2731
	FADEL	044	S-68		SIDI	076	S-75
ALI IBR. 017	MOSBAH	045	3234	ALHAMDEI 027	FARAG	077	3123
	ABDRZAK	046	3026		ARIBI	078	3100
	ALBAHLOL	047	2723		TAIB	079	2806
PRIBČINSKY 018	MUSTAFA	048	3228	PÁNEK 028	AMER	080	2750
	ALI	049	2857		TERFAS	081	2079
	LAROSSI	050	S-72		ODDAS	082	S-55
SALEM 019	ALAMORY	051	2719	ESMAIL 029	ENBARG	083	2906
	MOHAMED	052	3035		NASIR	084	2728
	SHEBA	053	2720		JOMA	085	3120

List of instructors and cadets of the 1st and 3rd Squadron of the 1st Training Wing at Okba ben Nafi air base in 1984. The code 'S' indicates cadets from abroad, in this case from Western Sahara. In addition, Algerians and Ugandans participated in pilot training as well. Libyan pilots were already serving as instructors during this period. (Miloslav Martenek via Miroslav Irra)

An L-39ZO of the LAAF underway during a training flight over central Libya. (Skalický via Miroslav Irra)

ASSESSMENT FROM THE CZECHOSLOVAK EMBASSY: 1979

The staff of the Czechoslovak embassy in Tripoli continued in the monitoring of developments within the Libyan Arab Armed Forces. The assessment of Libyan military capabilities in the year 1979 was as follows:

The Libyan armed forces have advanced their combat readiness, especially at the level of a battalion – an artillery battalion. Central command and top-down command remain a weak point. It is expected that it will be solved by a new organisation of the armed forces, which has already been partially addressed.

The battalion as a basic combat unit – tank or mechanised – advanced in its readiness mainly thanks to Czechoslovak and Soviet military experts. Thanks to them, these units are also able to perform combat missions. Logistics support still rests on battalions and limits their mobility.

Artillery battalions using material from socialist countries have also advanced in their readiness and are able to support the activities of the tank and mechanised units. It is also, although very rarely, carried out the cooperation of troops in exercises.

The level of readiness of special types of troops (engineers, signalmen, chemists) is very low and still rests mainly on their own forces or instructors trained abroad, especially in Western countries.

The country's air defence system is being intensively built under the leadership of Soviet military experts. Considerable progress has been made here.

The combat capability of the air force rests mainly on pilots trained on the Mirage who are supplemented by Pakistani pilots and others. Pilots trained in the Union of Soviet Socialist Republics on Soviet material are being improved and retrained on more modern Soviet aircraft with the help of Soviet experts.

In the autumn of 1978, the MUMKEN exercise was conducted with troops in cooperation with the air force and air defence force. It was a practical response to the planned aggression by the Arab Republic of Egypt. Its goal was to carry out defensive activities around the main coastal road in case of enemy assault. It turned out that the troops are not yet quite ready to carry out longer combat activities outside their own garrisons and to carry out their own logistical and technical support of this activity. Due to bad weather, the exercise had to be stopped, the troops in the Cyrenaica area were brought to the heights and supplied by helicopters. In this way, the exercise was also terminated.

[...]

The air force is a separate branch of the armed forces. It has its command elements and is directly subordinated to the commander-in-chief. However, its headquarters is very poorly staffed, numbering about 20 officers and dealing with only the most necessary issues of training and technical support. It is located at the Okba air base. Due to the limited number of officers of the headquarters, its influence in the units is very small.

The highest impact of assistance from abroad is evident in the air force. A limited number of air force officers have taken over command positions and only a small part remains in the squadrons as flying personnel. As a result, there are Pakistani specialists in virtually all units as technical personnel, as teachers in schools and courses, and as flying personnel operating the Mirage and Tu-22. Flying personnel from the Democratic People's Republic of Korea, which has about 120 persons, also occupy an important place. According to the findings, a large part was trained in the Union of Soviet Socialist Republics on the MiG-21 and participated in the 1973 War on the side of the Arab Republic of Egypt. There are 30 pilots and other technical personnel. There are also technicians and three pilots from South Yemen, four pilots and technicians from Bangladesh, two pilots – private individuals from the USA, flying on the Mirage.

There are also technical personnel for Mirage and helicopters from France and civilian technicians for Hercules aircraft, Sikorsky helicopters, Italian-made Bell helicopters, aircraft missiles and more.

[…]

The Aviation Technical Academy in Misurata, led by Yugoslav experts, has between 300 and 400 cadets a year, which also includes the training of aviation and technical personnel on the Yugoslav training aircraft Galeb. This Aviation Technical Academy, unlike Czechoslovak experts, trains officers. It is also realistically planned with 100 pilots – officers.

In the German Democratic Republic, 100 individuals are trained, half as pilots. The same number is in Yugoslavia and the Czechoslovak Socialist Republic. In addition, there are also flying personnel in various countries – especially Muslim ones.

[…]

The proficiency of Libyan pilots is still low, but it is progressing very quickly. It is also accelerating as the risk of conflict with the Arab Republic of Egypt grows. The preconditions for this are created both by the basis created by Mirages with the personnel and the now supplied Soviet technology, with which the relevant personnel is also trained. Nevertheless, the combat capability of the Libyan air force and its ability to perform combat missions is still determined by the presence of experts from abroad who largely perform combat tasks or these tasks are performed under their control.

[…]

The state air defence is a new headquarters created in 1978. It is very weakly staffed and its units are still under construction. It reports to the commander-in-chief. The air force has not yet incorporated part of its forces into the subordination of the air defence headquarters and therefore performs tasks in favour of air defence forces only at the request of the commander.

It is decided and the establishment of six air defence districts on the Mediterranean coast is underway. Each of these districts should have five to six battalions. So far, only the most important areas are secured, which are partly combat-ready, such as the area of Tobruk, Benghazi, Tripoli, in the initial stage it is in Sirte, Zuwarah, and Sebha. The core of the air defence establishment lies on Soviet specialists who make up more than half of the one thousand Soviet experts present.

[…]

The Libyan armed forces are currently focusing on the border with Egypt, where tensions are constantly escalating.

Recently, the area has been heavily fortified by Bulgarian and Turkish workers. There are built anti-tank and anti-infantry barricades and the line Bardiyah – Jaghbub is practically impenetrable by the enemy. Units deployed in this area were reinforced by a tank and mechanised battalion. The air defence brigade was also strengthened by one battalion. Part of the aviation wing with MiG-21s from Misurata was moved to Bomba. The navy at the Tobruk naval base was also strengthened, especially by patrol boats. Throughout this area, up to Bomba, there is a combat alert and troops are moved from the barracks, some of the officers go on holiday regularly. An aerial survey is being carried out intensively around the border from both sides. Otherwise, there is calm in this area.

Libyan troops in the number of 1,000 – 1,500 took part in a military expedition to Uganda in March and April 1979. They

Gaddafi – now wearing the rank of colonel – visiting the newly-constructed Ghurdabiya AB in the late 1970s. Barely visible in the background is a MiG-25 from No. 1055 Squadron. In 1979, the base also housed the LAAF's Syrte Air High School (formerly Tripoli Air High School) equipped with L-39ZOs, the operations of which were supported by a large team of Czechoslovak instructors. (Miloslav Martenek collection via Miroslav Irra)

were transported by Hercules and Il-76 aircraft of the Libyan air force. The Tu-22s bombed enemy targets in the early hours after an all-night flight from Kufra. One got lost in the action, fell into the jungle due to the loss of orientation.

Ground troops transported to the area were attacked before they could orient themselves and suffered significant losses and returned home within a few days. There is talk of losing up to 500 combatants.

The Libyan command has convinced itself that carrying out such tasks abroad requires mature consideration and evaluation of options.

Libyan troops are actively involved in combat operations in Chad. They are committed to supporting the various FROLINAT groups as they lean towards Libyan politics.

The northern part of Chad – a disputed territory – is occupied by Libyan regular troops. From there, the material is supplied and people are sent south, who return after two months to be replaced by others.

The base for activities in Chad is an oasis of Kufra and Sebha. Material and food for combatants in the south are transported from these places. Helicopters and trucks are used. Roads are already partly built to the south of these two places.

Conclusions:

The Libyan armed forces, as the country's main instrument of power and the pillar of the regime, are in a unique position. They report directly to the country's political leadership, which relies on them. Their numbers have increased significantly in the last year with calling up of 10 conscription grades, and it can be said that the armed forces now number about 75 thousand soldiers and officers.

[…]

Thus, the country's military preparedness has increased significantly in numbers, but the country's political and professional readiness is still weak. Social rifts in the army are beginning to emerge as a result of nationalisation measures, especially among officers. The calling up of thousands of employees and small tradesmen is supposed to get rid of this large class, but it greatly increases dissatisfaction in the armed forces. The growth of numbers in the army is crippling the course of civilian life. The manifestation of any dissatisfaction in the armed forces is being severely liquidated.

[…]

It can be assumed that with the assistance of military experts from socialist countries, the Libyan armed forces would be able to repel the enemy's attack.[50]

BIBLIOGRAPHY

ARCHIVE SOURCES

Archiv Ministerstva zahraničních věcí (AMZV), Praha (Archive of the Ministry of Foreign Affairs, Prague)

Fond Teritoriální odbory - tajné (TO-T), 1955-1959 (Fund Teritorial Departments - Secret, 1955-1959)

Fond Teritoriální odbory - tajné (TO-T), 1970-1974 (Fund Teritorial Departments - Secret, 1970-1974)

Fond Teritoriální odbory - tajné (TO-T), 1975-1979 (Fund Teritorial Departments - Secret, 1975-1979)

Fond Teritoriální odbory - tajné (TO-T), 1980-1989 (Fund Teritorial Departments - Secret, 1980-1989)

Národní archiv (NA), Praha (National Archive, Prague)

Fond Politické byro ÚV KSČ 1954-1962, 1261/0/11 (Fund Political Bureau ÚV KSČ 1954-1962, 1261/0/11)

Fond Předsednictvo ÚV KSČ 1962-1966, 1261/0/4 (Fund Presidium ÚV KSČ 1962-1966, 1261/0/4)

Fond Předsednictvo ÚV KSČ 1966-1971, 1261/0/5 (Fund Presidium ÚV KSČ 1966-1971, 1261/0/5)

Fond Předsednictvo ÚV KSČ 1971-1976, 1261/0/6 (Fund Presidium ÚV KSČ 1971-1976, 1261/0/6)

Fond Předsednictvo ÚV KSČ 1976-1981, 1261/0/7 (Fund Presidium ÚV KSČ 1976-1981, 1261/0/7)

Fond Předsednictvo ÚV KSČ 1981-1986, 1261/0/8 (Fund Presidium ÚV KSČ 1981-1986, 1261/0/8)

Fond Předsednictvo ÚV KSČ 1986-1989, 1261/0/9 (Fund Presidium ÚV KSČ 1986-1989, 1261/0/9)

Fond Kancelář 1. tajemníka ÚV KSČ Antonína Novotného - II. část, 1261/0/44 (Fund Office of First Secretary ÚV KSČ Antonín Novotný - II part, 1261/0/44)

Vojenský ústřední archiv - Vojenský historický archiv (VÚA-VHA), Praha (Military Central Archive - Military Historical Archive, Prague)

Fond Ministerstvo národní obrany (MNO), 1951-1980 (Fund Ministry of National Defence, 1951-1980)

DIPLOMA THESES

Borovský, Matyáš, *Podání ruky "vzteklému psu Blízkého východu": vztahy mezi Kaddáfího Libyí a Východním blokem na příkladu ČSSR* (Praha: Filozofická fakulta, Univerzita Karlova, 2020)

Vyhlídal, Milan, Československá *pomoc při výstavbě vojenského školství v arabském světě* v *letech 1948 - 1989* (Brno: Filozofická fakulta, Masarykova univerzita, 2010)

LITERATURE

Fojtík, Jakub, *Albatros. AERO L-39, L-59, L-139* (Bratislava: Magnet Press Slovakia, 2016)

Francev, Vladimír, *Československé zbraně ve světě* (Praha: Grada Publishing, 2015)

Francev, Vladimír, *Československé tankové síly* (Praha: Grada Publishing, 2012)

Irra, Miroslav, *L-39 Albatros, 2. díl* (Nevojice: Jakab, 2017)

Irra, Miroslav, *L-39 Albatros, 3. díl* (Nevojice: Jakab, 2017)

Stojanov, Robert, *Finanční pohledávky České republiky u rozvojových zemí* (Praha: Ekumenická akademie, 2019)

Zídek, Petr & Sieber, Karel, Československo *a Blízký východ v letech 1948-1989* (Praha: *Ústav* mezinárodních vztahů, 2009)

PERIODICALS

Baka, Igor, *Československá* vojenská pomoc Líbyi v 70. rokoch 20. storočia, *Vojenská história*, 1/2012

Baka, Igor, Československá vojenská pomoc Líbyi v prvej polovici osmdesiatych rokoch dvadsiateho storočia, *Vojenská história*, 3/2012

Baka, Igor, *Československá* vojenská pomoc Líbyi v druhej polovici osemdesiatych rokov 20. storočia, *Vojenská história*, 4/2012

Štaigl, Jan & Turza, Peter, Zbrojná výroba na Slovensku v rokoch 1969-1992 (1. časť), *Vojenská história*, 2/2013

Štaigl, Jan & Turza, Peter, Zbrojná výroba na Slovensku v rokoch 1969-1992 (2. časť), *Vojenská história*, 3/2013

Žáček, Pavel, Vojenské zpravodajství z Libye a terorismus. Rezidentura „Ropa" v materiálech Hlavní správy vojenské kontrarozvědky, *Paměť a dějiny*, 3/2011

INTERNET

explosia.cz

www.leteckabadatelna.cz

www.mfcr.cz

www.valka.cz

ENDNOTES

Chapter 1

1. Zídek & Sieber, Československo a Blízký východ v letech 1948-1989, pp.21–22.
2. NA, A ÚV KSČ, Politické byro ÚV KSČ 1954-1962 (1261/0/11), sv. 130, ar.j. 170, bod 15, Schůze PB ÚV KSČ ze dne 26.2.1957. NA, A ÚV KSČ, fond 1261/0/44 (Kancelář 1. tajemníka ÚV KSČ Antonína Novotného - II. část), karton 70 (Alžírsko), inv. č. 71, obal 16a, Zpráva MV o dodávkách československých zbraní do Alžírska, 1958. VÚA-VHA, MNO, 1957, karton 397, sign. 30/2, č.j. 00232/4/SMP-57, dodávky vojenské techniky do Maroka, 9. března 1957. VÚA-VHA, MNO, 1957, karton 397, sign. 30/2, k č.j. 00232/14-SMP-5, Uvolnění materiálu pro vývoz, 16. květen 1957. Zídek & Sieber, Československo a Blízký východ v letech 1948-1989, pp.24–25.
3. VÚA-VHA, MNO, 1957, karton 396, sign. 30-2/94, Dodávkové příkazy dělostřeleckého materiálu ze skladů.
4. NA, A ÚV KSČ, fond 1261/0/44 (Kancelář 1. tajemníka ÚV KSČ Antonína Novotného - II. část), karton 70 (Alžírsko), inv. č. 71, obal 16a, Zpráva MV o dodávkách československých zbraní do Alžírska, 1958. VÚA-VHA, MNO, 1957, karton 397, sign. 30/2, k č.j. 00232/13-SMP-5, dodávka speciálního materiálu prostřednictvím Jugoslávie, 2. května 1957. Zídek & Sieber, Československo a Blízký východ v letech 1948-1989, pp.24–25.
5. VÚA-VHA, MNO, 1957, karton 396, sign. 30-2/94, Dodávkové příkazy dělostřeleckého materiálu ze skladů. VÚA-VHA, MNO, 1962, karton 367, sign. 30-2/4, Souhrnné dokumenty o vývozu, Přehled o vývozu vojenské techniky do kapitalistických států, 6. února 1959. VÚA-VHA, MNO, 1969, karton 172, Evidence GŠ/SMP-5 – vývozní skupina. VÚA-VHA, MNO, 1969, karton 173, Evidence GŠ/SMP-5 – vývozní skupina.
6. NA, A ÚV KSČ, fond 1261/0/44 (Kancelář 1. tajemníka ÚV KSČ Antonína Novotného - II. část), karton 70 (Alžírsko), inv. č. 71, obal 16a, Zpráva MV o dodávkách československých zbraní do Alžírska, 1958. Zídek & Sieber, *Československo a Blízký východ v letech 1948-1989*, pp.25–26, 299.
7. VÚA-VHA, MNO, 1962, karton 367, sign. 30-2/4, Souhrnné dokumenty o vývozu, Přehled o vývozu vojenské techniky do kapitalistických států, 6. února 1959. VÚA-VHA, MNO, 1969, karton 172, Evidence GŠ/SMP-5 – vývozní skupina. VÚA-VHA, MNO, 1969, karton 173, Evidence GŠ/SMP-5 – vývozní skupina.
8. VÚA-VHA, MNO, 1958, karton 366, sign. 30-2/3/59, č.j. 0012982, Uvolnění materiálu pro Maroko, 3. prosince 1958. VÚA-VHA, MNO, 1967, karton 28, sl. 2/7/1-10, č.j. 055184-20, Zpráva o účasti čs. voj. delegace v Maroku, 30. listopadu 1967. Zídek & Sieber, Československo a Blízký východ v letech 1948-1989, p.26.
9. VÚA-VHA, MNO, 1958, karton 366, sign. 30-2/3/59, č.j. 0012982, Uvolnění materiálu pro Maroko, 3. prosince 1958. VÚA-VHA, MNO, 1969, karton 172, Evidence GŠ/SMP-5 – vývozní skupina. VÚA-VHA, MNO, 1969, karton 173, Evidence GŠ/SMP-5 – vývozní skupina.
10. VÚA-VHA, MNO, 1958, karton 366, sign. 30-2/3/59, č.j. 0012982, Uvolnění materiálu pro Maroko, 3. prosince 1958. VÚA-VHA, MNO, 1969, karton 172, Evidence GŠ/SMP-5 – vývozní skupina. VÚA-VHA, MNO, 1969, karton 173, Evidence GŠ/SMP-5 – vývozní skupina.
11. NA, A ÚV KSČ, Politické byro ÚV KSČ 1954-1962 (1261/0/11), sv. 194, ar.j. 265, bod 17, Dodávka trofejní vojenské techniky do Maroka přes zprostředkovatele, 1. listopadu 1958. NA, A ÚV KSČ, Politické byro ÚV KSČ 1954-1962 (1261/0/11), sv. 215, ar.j. 292, bod 2, Nedostatky při dodávce speciální techniky lodí „Lidice" do Maroka, 25. dubna 1959. Zídek & Sieber, Československo a Blízký východ v letech 1948-1989, pp.26–29.
12. NA, A ÚV KSČ, Politické byro ÚV KSČ 1954-1962 (1261/0/11), sv. 218-219, ar.j. 297, bod 4, Opatření k odstranění závad zjištěných při dodávce speciální techniky lodí „Lidice" do Maroka, 29. května 1959. NA, A ÚV KSČ, Politické byro ÚV KSČ 1954-1962 (1261/0/11), sv. 225, ar.j. 305, bod 9, Náhradní dodávka vojenské techniky marockému ministerstvu národní obrany, 18. července 1959. NA, A ÚV KSČ, fond 1261/0/44 (Kancelář 1. tajemníka ÚV KSČ Antonína Novotného - II. část), karton 135 (Maroko), inv. č. 315, obal 21, Zpráva o jednání dr. Zachystala v Maroku (zadržení lodi Lidice, jednání s ministerským předsedou, MZV, MZO, dodávky zbraní, otázka diplomatických styků), 1959. VÚA-VHA, MNO, 1959, karton 350, sign. 30-2/141, č.j. 007906/SMP-5, Náhradní dodávky vojenské techniky pro Maroko, 22. července 1959.
13. VÚA-VHA, MNO, 1969, karton 172, Evidence GŠ/SMP-5 – vývozní skupina.
14. NA, A ÚV KSČ, Politické byro ÚV KSČ 1954-1962 (1261/0/11), sv. 301, ar.j. 385, bod 11, Pomoc prozatimní alžírské vládě, 22. března 1961. NA, A ÚV KSČ, fond 1261/0/44 (Kancelář 1. tajemníka ÚV KSČ Antonína Novotného - II. část), karton 70 (Alžírsko), inv. č. 71, obal 19, Návštěva představitelů PV AR v ČSSR, 1961. NA, A ÚV KSČ, fond 1261/0/44 (Kancelář 1. tajemníka ÚV KSČ Antonína Novotného - II. část), karton 209 (Svaz sovětských socialistických republik), inv. č. 189, obal 432, Dohoda mezi SSSR a ČSSR o vzájemných dodávkách vojenského materiálu (roční a dlouhodobé dohody) – Záznam z jednání ředitele hlavní technické správy MZO s. Mareše s generálem Sidorovičem a plukovníkem Sergejčikem v Moskvě ve dnech 18.-20. března 1961, 1961. VÚA-VHA, MNO, 1961, karton 450, sign. 30-2/5/19, č.j. 0015555/NGŠ-61, Dodávky speciálního materiálu pro alžírskou osvobozeneckou armádu, 21. února 1961.
15. NA, A ÚV KSČ, Politické byro ÚV KSČ 1954-1962 (1261/0/11), sv. 301, ar.j. 385, bod 11, Pomoc prozatimní alžírské vládě, 22. března 1961. VÚA-VHA, MNO, 1961, karton 449, sign. 30-2/114, č.j. 0011895/SMP-5, Zpráva o plnění dodávek voj. mat. armádám hospodářsky málo vyvinutých zemí, 28. července 1961. VÚA-VHA, MNO, 1961, karton 457, sign. 33-2/44, č.j. 0011009/SMP-5, Dodávka voj. mat. prozatimní vládě Alžírské republiky, 23. červen 1961. VÚA-VHA, MNO, 1969, karton 172, Evidence GŠ/SMP-5 – vývozní skupina. VÚA-VHA, MNO, 1969, karton 173, Evidence GŠ/SMP-5 – vývozní skupina. VÚA-VHA, MNO, 1969, karton 175, Evidence GŠ/SMP-5 – vývozní skupina. VÚA-VHA, MNO, 1969, karton 176, Evidence GŠ/SMP-5 – vývozní skupina.
16. NA, A ÚV KSČ, fond 1261/0/44 (Kancelář 1. tajemníka ÚV KSČ Antonína Novotného - II. část), karton 70 (Alžírsko), inv. č. 71, obal 19, Návštěva představitelů PV AR v ČSSR, 1961. NA, A ÚV KSČ, fond 1261/0/44 (Kancelář 1. tajemníka ÚV KSČ Antonína Novotného - II. část), karton 93 (Egypt), inv. č. 142, obal 51, Telegramy, šifry, depeše ZÚ. VÚA-VHA, MNO, 1961, karton 457, sign. 33-2/44, č.j. 0011009/SMP-5, Dodávka voj. mat. prozatimní vládě Alžírské republiky, 23. červen 1961.
17. NA, A ÚV KSČ, fond 1261/0/44 (Kancelář 1. tajemníka ÚV KSČ Antonína Novotného - II. část), karton 70 (Alžírsko), inv. č. 71, obal 19, Návštěva představitelů PV AR v ČSSR, 1961. VÚA-VHA, MNO, 1961, karton 457, sign. 33-2/44, č.j. 0011009/SMP-5, Dodávka voj. mat. prozatimní vládě Alžírské republiky, 23. červen 1961. VÚA-VHA, MNO, 1962, karton 376, sign. G/27, Návrh technické pomoci Alžírské armádě v oblasti pozemních specialistů.
18. NA, A ÚV KSČ, Politické byro ÚV KSČ 1954-1962 (1261/0/11), sv. 310, ar.j. 394, bod 12, Další požadavky Bulharské lidové republiky na speciální materiál, 9. června 1961. VÚA-VHA, MNO, 1961, karton 449, sign. 30/2/1, Dodávkové příkazy na rok 1961.
19. NA, A ÚV KSČ, fond 1261/0/44 (Kancelář 1. tajemníka ÚV KSČ Antonína Novotného - II. část), karton 223 (Tunisko), inv. č. 535, obal 14, Telegramy, zprávy, šifry ZÚ, 1962.

20 VÚA-VHA, MNO, 1968, karton 62, sl. 30-3/3, Výkazy jmenovitých
    položek za I. – IV. čtvrtletí 1962, 2. února 1963.
21 VÚA-VHA, MNO, 1962, karton 287, sign. 31/2/30, č. 011.728/62,
    Zpráva o pobytu čs. vládní delegace na oslavách státního svát-
    ku Alžírské demokratické lidové republiky, 27. listopadu 1962.
    VÚA-VHA, MNO, 1963, karton 361, sign. G/27, Materiální pomoc
    Alžírsku, 23. října 1963.
22 NA, A ÚV KSČ, Politické byro ÚV KSČ 1954-1962 (1261/0/11),
    sv. 338, ar.j. 428, bod 26, Výcvik alžírských leteckých odborníků
    v ČSSR, 9. února 1962. NA, A ÚV KSČ, fond 1261/0/44 (Kancelář
    1. tajemníka ÚV KSČ Antonína Novotného - II. část), karton
    70 (Alžírsko), inv. č. 71, obal 22, Výcvik alžírských leteckých
    odborníků v ČSSR, 1962. VÚA-VHA, MNO, 1962, karton 25,
    sign. S/3-125, č.j. 0013275/24a-1961, Výcvik alžírských vojenských
    leteckých techniků v ČSSR, 18. dubna 1962.
23 VÚA-VHA, MNO, 1962, karton 376, sign. G/20, č.j. 0013275/
    OTP, Vyloučení 2 alžírských posluchačů z leteckého výcviku, 6
    .července 1962. VÚA-VHA, MNO, 1963, karton 87, sign. 38-3-122,
    č.j. 029014-50, Hlášení o ukončení kursu A-130/225, 22. prosinec
    1963.
24 VÚA-VHA, MNO, 1962, karton 376, sign. G/27, Seznam alžír-
    ských žáků. VÚA-VHA, MNO, 1964, karton 326, sign. G/1, č.j.
    03102/43, Zpráva o ukončení kursu alžírských leteckých techniků,
    10. února 1964. VÚA-VHA, MNO, 1964, karton 327, sign. G/4, č.j.
    1124--/43, Ukončení léčby absolventa let. výcv. střediska Babahadi,
    březen 1964.
25 NA, A ÚV KSČ, fond 1261/0/44 (Kancelář 1. tajemníka ÚV KSČ
    Antonína Novotného - II. část), karton 70 (Alžírsko), inv. č. 71,
    obal 26, Pozvání vojenské delegace ALDR k návštěvě ČSSR, 1962.
    VÚA-VHA, MNO, 1963, karton 361, sign. G/3, č.j. 02076/OTP,
    Školení 12 alžírských posluchačů A-130, kurs 235, 13. únor 1963.
26 VÚA-VHA, MNO, 1963, karton 361, sign. G/12, č.j. 02139, Opis
    zprávy, 22. března 1963. VÚA-VHA, MNO, 1963, karton 361,
    sign. G/15, č.j. 023038/50, Vyloučení žáka Mohameda Gheraia
    z kursu č. 235, 7. květen 1963. VÚA-VHA, MNO, 1963, karton
    361, sign. G/18, č.j. 01490-30-63, Přijetí zahraničních studentů ke
    studiu na VA AZ ve škol. Roce 1963/1964, 3. července 1963. VÚA-
    VHA, MNO, 1963, karton 361, sign. G/26, č.j. 026942, Hlášení o
    ukončení kursu A-130/235, 5. říjen 1963. VÚA-VHA, MNO, 1964,
    karton 326, sign. K/10, č.j. 003076/OTP, Souhrnná zpráva o posky-
    tování technické pomoci HMVZ za rok 1963, únor 1964.
27 VÚA-VHA, MNO, 1967, karton 163, sl. 31G-20, č.j. 5769/17, Zprá-
    va o ukončení inž. školení alžírských posluchačů, říjen 1967.
28 NA, A ÚV KSČ, fond 1261/0/44 (Kancelář 1. tajemníka ÚV KSČ
    Antonína Novotného - II. část), karton 70 (Alžírsko), inv. č. 71,
    obal 29, Informace o československo-alžírské spolupráci ve vojen-
    ské oblasti, 1964.
29 NA, A ÚV KSČ, fond 1261/0/44 (Kancelář 1. tajemníka ÚV KSČ
    Antonína Novotného - II. část), karton 70 (Alžírsko), inv. č. 71,
    obal 46, Telegramy, zprávy, šifry ZÚ, 1963. VÚA-VHA, MNO,
    1963, karton 361, sign. G/27, č.j. 02522-OTP-1963, Výstrojní
    materiál pro Alžírskou demokratickou lidovou republiku, 29. října
    1963.
30 Zídek & Sieber, Československo a Blízký východ v letech 1948-
    1989, pp.41–43.
31 VÚA-VHA, MNO, 1965, karton 160, sign. 31/2/2, č.j.026668 GŠ/
    ZS, Hodnocení současné situace v Alžírsku, 8. července 1965.
32 VÚA-VHA, MNO, 1975, karton 146, sign. 01001 (V), č.j. 001101/
    SÚP-1975, Informace o čs. – alžírských vztazích ve speciální oblas-
    ti.
33 Zídek & Sieber, Československo a Blízký východ v letech 1948-
    1989, pp.41–43.
34 VÚA-VHA, MNO, 1974, karton 120, sl. 84/14, č.j. 008069/12-
    FMNO/14-1974, Přehled zahraničních odběratelů speciálního
    materiálu z ČSSR v letech 1970-1974.
35 NA, A ÚV KSČ, fond 1261/0/7 (Předsednictvo ÚV KSČ 1976-
    1981), sv. 82, ar.j. 85, bod 5, Zpráva o požadavcích vlády Alžírské
    demokratické a lidové republiky na dodávky speciálního materiá-
    lu, 18. září 1978.
36 Francev, Československé tankové síly, p.163. Štaigl & Turza, Zbrojná
    výroba na Slovensku v rokoch 1969-1992 (2. časť), p.91.
37 NA, A ÚV KSČ, fond 1261/0/7 (Předsednictvo ÚV KSČ 1976-
    1981), sv. 82, ar.j. 85, bod 5, Zpráva o požadavcích vlády Alžírské
    demokratické a lidové republiky na dodávky speciálního materiá-
    lu, 18. září 1978.
38 AMZV, TO-T 1980-1989, Alžírsko, karton 1, obal 3, č.j.
    030982/021-84, Informace o vztazích ve speciální oblasti s ALDR,
    10. července 1984. AMZV, TO-T 1980-1989, Alžírsko, karton 1,
    obal 6, č.j. 012160/92-81, Informace o vztazích s Alžírskem ve
    speciální oblasti, 30. ledna 1981.
39 Ibid.
40 NA, A ÚV KSČ, fond 1261/0/8 (Předsednictvo ÚV KSČ 1981-
    1986), P 15/86, bod 19, Zpráva o řešení požadavku Alžírské
    demokratické a lidové republiky na poskytnutí dalšího úvěru
    ve speciální oblasti, 5. září 1986. NA, A ÚV KSČ, fond 1261/0/9
    (Předsednictvo ÚV KSČ 1986-1989), P 61/88, bod 1/a, b, Zpráva
    o plnění závěrů z návštěvy generálního tajemníka ÚV KSČ a
    prezidenta ČSSR s. G. HUSÁKA v Alžírské demokratické a lidové
    republice v září 1986, 11. února 1988.
41 Francev, Československé tankové síly, p.163. Francev, Československé
    zbraně ve světě, p.158. Štaigl & Turza, Zbrojná výroba na Slovensku
    v rokoch 1969-1992 (2. časť), p.91.
42 Fojtík, Albatros, pp.87–90.
43 Irra, L-39 Albatros, 2. díl, pp.33–34.
44 Stojanov, Finanční pohledávky České republiky u rozvojových zemí,
    p.16.

Chapter 2
1 Zídek & Sieber, Československo a Blízký východ v letech 1948-
   1989, pp.178–179.
2 NA, A ÚV KSČ, fond 1261/0/44 (Kancelář 1. tajemníka ÚV KSČ
   Antonína Novotného - II. část), karton 135 (Maroko), inv. č. 315,
   obal 32, Telegramy a šifry ZÚ 1959-1960 (1963).
3 VÚA-VHA, MNO, 1964, karton 22, sign. 24/5/1-30, č.j. 0050928/
   HTS-05, Zpráva o výsledcích průzkumu možností odbytu speciálního materiálu, 30. června 1964. VÚA-VHA, MNO, 1964, karton
   26, sign. 39/1-5, č.j. 0010787/sekr.MNO-1964, Uvolnění tankové
   munice pro Maroko, 16. března 1964.
4 NA, A ÚV KSČ, fond 1261/0/5 (Předsednictvo ÚV KSČ 1966-
   1971), sv. 34, ar.j. 36, bod 2, Zájem Maroka o nákup speciální
   techniky v Československu, 31. května 1967. VÚA-VHA, MNO,
   1967, karton 160, sl. 31/G, k č.j. 01919/SZS-1967, Informační
   materiál pro jednání náčelníka gen. štábu s marockou voj. delegací
   dne 22.6.1967 v 11.00 hod. ve Slunné 15.
5 NA, A ÚV KSČ, fond 1261/0/5 (Předsednictvo ÚV KSČ 1966-
   1971), sv. 34, ar.j. 36, bod 2, Zájem Maroka o nákup speciální
   techniky v Československu, 31. května 1967. NA, A ÚV KSČ, fond
   1261/0/5 (Předsednictvo ÚV KSČ 1966-1971), sv. 42, ar.j. 43, bod
   12, Zpráva o uzavření dohody na dodávky speciálních materiálů
   z Československa do Maroka a návrh dalšího postupu, 11. srpna
   1967.
6 NA, A ÚV KSČ, fond 1261/0/5 (Předsednictvo ÚV KSČ 1966-
   1971), sv. 42, ar.j. 43, bod 12, Zpráva o uzavření dohody na
   dodávky speciálních materiálů z Československa do Maroka a
   návrh dalšího postupu, 11. srpna 1967. VÚA-VHA, MNO, 1967,
   karton 161, sl.31/L/98, Dodávkové příkazy ročník 1967.
7 NA, A ÚV KSČ, fond 1261/0/5 (Předsednictvo ÚV KSČ 1966-
   1971), sv. 42, ar.j. 43, bod 12, Zpráva o uzavření dohody na
   dodávky speciálních materiálů z Československa do Maroka a
   návrh dalšího postupu, 11. srpna 1967. VÚA-VHA, MNO, 1967,
   karton 35, sl. 24/5/2-7, č.j. 02419/SZS, Materiál pro přijetí marocké
   delegace, 11. září 1967. VÚA-VHA, MNO, 1967, karton 160, sl.
   31/G, Sběrný arch Akce 199 – Maroko. VÚA-VHA, MNO, 1967,
   karton 161, sl.31/L/98, Dodávkové příkazy ročník 1967.

8   VÚA-VHA, MNO, 1967, karton 160, sl. 31/G, Sběrný arch Akce 199 – Maroko. VÚA-VHA, MNO, 1967, karton 161, sl.31/L/98, Dodávkové příkazy ročník 1967.

9   VÚA-VHA, MNO, 1968, karton 80, sl. 22/1, č.j. 012297/68, Komplexní rozbor zahraničních styků ministerstva národní obrany, uskutečněných v roce 1967, 11. března 1968. VÚA-VHA, MNO, 1969, karton 27, sl. 7/1-1, č.j. 020659, Komplexní rozbor zahraničních styků ministerstva národní obrany, uskutečněných v roce 1968, 28. března 1969. VÚA-VHA, MNO, 1970, karton 143, sl. 30 (H), k č.j. 9364-MNO/SZS.

10 VÚA-VHA, MNO, 1967, karton 160, sl. 31G-33, č.j. 02984/17, Zpráva o školení K 199 A – zaslání, prosinec 1967. VÚA-VHA, MNO, 1968, karton 80, sl. 22/1, č.j. 012297/68, Komplexní rozbor zahraničních styků ministerstva národní obrany uskutečněných v roce 1967, 11. března 1968.

11 VÚA-VHA, MNO, 1967, karton 160, sl. 31G-33, č.j. 02984/17, Zpráva o školení K 199 A – zaslání, prosinec 1967.

12 VÚA-VHA, MNO, 1967, karton 28, sl. 2/7/1-10, č.j. 055184-20, Zpráva o účasti čs. voj. delegace v Maroku, 30. listopadu 1967. VÚA-VHA, MNO, 1968, karton 84, sl. 31G-7, č.j. 46582, Vrácení zprávy vedoucího čs. expertů v Maroku, 9. ledna 1968. VÚA-VHA, MNO, 1969, karton 27, sl. 7/1-1, č.j. 020659, Komplexní rozbor zahraničních styků ministerstva národní obrany, uskutečněných v roce 1968, 28. března 1969.

13 VÚA-VHA, MNO, 1969, karton 27, sl. 7/1-1, č.j. 020659, Komplexní rozbor zahraničních styků ministerstva národní obrany, uskutečněných v roce 1968, 28. března 1969.

14 Within the frame of the federalisation of Czechoslovakia, the Czech Socialist Republic and the Slovak Socialist Republic were established on 1 January 1969. This was associated with renaming of ministries with statewide authority that earned the word Federal into their official titles.

15 VÚA-VHA, MNO, 1968, karton 84, sl. 31G-45, č.j. 10553/17, Školení marockých odborníků v ČSSR, prosinec 1968. VÚA-VHA, MNO, 1969, karton 207, sl. 50/9, č.j. 7117, Zpráva o průběhu školení marockých odborníků. VÚA-VHA, MNO, 1969, karton 215, sl. 31G-27, č.j. 17648/SZS, Zpráva o průběhu marockých kursů, srpen 1969. VÚA-VHA, MNO, 1969, karton 215, sl. 31G-36, č.j. 18336/17, Zpráva o ukončení kursu marockých odborníků, 30. září 1969. VÚA-VHA, MNO, 1970, karton 153, sl. 31-7/4, č.j. 20968, Hodnocení kursů 290, 291, 292 – Maroko, 24. března 1970.

16 VÚA-VHA, MNO, 1969, karton 201, sl. 30/3, Plán vývozních úkolů a předpokládané příjmy MNO pro r. 1970. VÚA-VHA, MNO, 1969, karton 207, sl. 50/31, č.j. 12434, Smlouva mezi VA AZ-ZF a OZ 026 Šternberk – opis, 8. prosince 1969.

17 VÚA-VHA, MNO, 1968, karton 84, sl. 31G-45, č.j. 10553/17, Školení marockých odborníků v ČSSR, prosinec 1968. VÚA-VHA, MNO, 1970, karton 137, sl. 12/21, č.j. 012152, Zaslání výroční zprávy ZF za rok 1969, 5. ledna 1970.

18 VÚA-VHA, MNO, 1970, karton 153, sl. 31-4/57, č.j. 8560, Opravny v Sudanu, Iraku a Maroku, duben 1970. VÚA-VHA, MNO, 1971, karton 138, sl. 12/25, č.j. 03012/8, Předání materiálů, 8. září 1971.

19 Zídek & Sieber, Československo a Blízký východ v letech 1948-1989, pp.227–230.

20 VÚA-VHA, MNO, 1974, karton 120, sl. 84/14, č.j. 008069/12-FMNO/14-1974, Přehled zahraničních odběratelů speciálního materiálu z ČSSR v letech 1970-1974.

Chapter 3

1   Zídek & Sieber, Československo a Blízký východ v letech 1948-1989, pp.190–192.

2   VÚA-VHA, MNO, 1967, karton 161, sl. 31/L98, Dodávkové příkazy ročník 1967.

3   Zídek & Sieber, Československo a Blízký východ v letech 1948-1989, pp.193–194.

4   NA, A ÚV KSČ, fond 1261/0/7 (Předsednictvo ÚV KSČ 1976-1981), sv. 42, ar.j. 47, bod 15, Zpráva o požadavcích Libye na dodávky a technickou pomoc ve speciální oblasti, 16. června 1977.

5   VÚA-VHA, MNO, 1974, karton 120, sl. 84/14, č.j. 008069/12-FMNO/14-1974, Přehled zahraničních odběratelů speciálního materiálu z ČSSR v letech 1970-1974.

6   Zídek & Sieber, Československo a Blízký východ v letech 1948-1989, pp.195–196.

7   VÚA-VHA, MNO, 1973, karton 100, sl. 53/3, Akce 99 – přehled písemností, Informační zpráva k situaci v řešení požadavků o pomoc arabským zemím. Zídek & Sieber, Československo a Blízký východ v letech 1948-1989, pp.198–199.

8   VÚA-VHA, MNO, 1973, karton 101, sl. 85/14, k č.j. 0016693-2/23-73, AKCE 98, ZPRÁVA ze služební cesty v TRIPOLI – LIBYE, 31. října 1973.

9   Zídek & Sieber, Československo a Blízký východ v letech 1948-1989, p.198.

10 NA, A ÚV KSČ, fond 1261/0/6 (Předsednictvo ÚV KSČ 1971-1976), sv. 110, ar.j. 112, bod 10, Zpráva o návštěvě člena Vojenské revoluční rady a předsedy vlády Libyjské arabské republiky Abdel Salám Džalúda v ČSSR, 1. března 1974.

11 Baka, *Československá vojenská pomoc Líbyi v 70. rokoch 20. storočia*, pp.56–57.

12 VÚA-VHA, MNO, 1975, karton 101, sl. 41/10, č.j. 001964, Zpráva o čs.-libyjských vztazích ve speciální obchodní oblasti, 14. srpna 1975.

13 Ibid. VÚA-VHA, MNO, 1975, karton 12, sl. 84/1, k č.j. 01187/SÚP-1975, Odprodej výrobní licenční dokumentace Libyi a Peru, únor 1975. Baka, *Československá vojenská pomoc Líbyi v 70. rokoch 20. storočia*, p.57.

14 VÚA-VHA, MNO, 1974, karton 120, sl. 85/15, č.j. 0185683/06, Zpráva o dalších požadavcích Libyjské arabské republiky na dodávky tanků z ČSSR do Libye v letech 1976-1977, 15. srpna 1974.

15 According to Baka, *Československá vojenská pomoc Líbyi v 70. rokoch 20. storočia* (p.70), 91 Libyans arrived in Czechoslovakia.

16 NA, A ÚV KSČ, fond 1261/0/6 (Předsednictvo ÚV KSČ 1971-1976), sv. 167, ar.j. 168, k informaci bod 4, Zpráva o požadavku Libyjské arabské republiky na výcvik libyjského personálu v ČSSR. NA, A ÚV KSČ, fond 1261/0/7 (Předsednictvo ÚV KSČ 1976-1981), sv. 42, ar.j. 47, bod 15, Zpráva o požadavcích Libye na dodávky a technickou pomoc ve speciální oblasti, 16. června 1977. VÚA-VHA, MNO, 1975, karton 101, sl. 41/10, č.j. 001964, Zpráva o čs.-libyjských vztazích ve speciální obchodní oblasti, 14. srpna 1975.

17 AMZV, TO-T 1975-1979, Libye, karton 1, obal 2, č.j. 01106/76, Informace o armádě LAR, 21. dubna 1976.

18 NA, A ÚV KSČ, fond 1261/0/6 (Předsednictvo ÚV KSČ 1971-1976), sv. 172, ar.j. 174, bod 21, Zpráva o návštěvě předsedy vlády ČSSR s. L. Štrougala v Libyjské arabské republice ve dnech 13.-15. března 1975, 28. října 1975.

19 AMZV, TO-T 1975-1979, Libye, karton 1, obal 3, č.j. 01189/77, Libye – vztahy se ZSS ve vojenské oblasti, 10. srpna 1977.

20 AMZV, TO-T 1975-1979, Libye, karton 3, obal 3, č.j. 017.274/77-8, Informační materiál k přijetí nového libyjského velvyslance Ramadán Mustafy Saláha, březen 1978.

21 NA, A ÚV KSČ, fond 1261/0/7 (Předsednictvo ÚV KSČ 1976-1981), sv. 42, ar.j. 47, bod 15, Zpráva o požadavcích Libye na dodávky a technickou pomoc ve speciální oblasti, 16. června 1977.

22 Ibid. VÚA-VHA, MNO, 1980, karton 143, č.j. 022543/v, Zpráva o činnosti průz. skupiny v LAR – předložení, 29. července 1977. VÚA-VHA, MNO, 1980, karton 183, č.j. 381, č.j. 0011772-84, Podklad pro jednání PV ČSSR, 27. května 1977.

23 Ibid.

24 AMZV, TO-T 1975-1979, Libye, karton 1, obal 3, č.j. 01189/77, Libye – vztahy se ZSS ve vojenské oblasti, 10. srpna 1977.

25 NA, A ÚV KSČ, fond 1261/0/7 (Předsednictvo ÚV KSČ 1976-1981), sv. 42, ar.j. 47, bod 15, Zpráva o požadavcích Libye na dodávky a technickou pomoc ve speciální oblasti, 16. června 1977.

26 VÚA-VHA, MNO, 1977, karton 121, č.j. 06974, Akce Litomyšl – V 1650/737.

27 Ibid.

28 Ibid.

29 NA, A ÚV KSČ, fond 1261/0/7 (Předsednictvo ÚV KSČ 1976-1981), sv. 62, ar.j. 66, k informaci bod 3, Informace o průběhu a výsledcích návštěvy ministra zahraničních věcí ČSSR B. Chňoupka v Libyjské arabské lidové socialistické džamahiriji ve dnech 11. – 16. prosince 1977, 9. ledna 1978.

30 VÚA-VHA, MNO, 1977, karton 121, č.j. 06974, Akce Litomyšl – V 1650/737.

31 VÚA-VHA, MNO, 1978, karton 214, č.j. 08226, Technická pomoc v opravně TOBRUK – Libye.

32 AMZV, TO-T 1975-1979, Libye, karton 5, obal 24, č.j. 01140/78, Libye- libyjské ozbrojené síly, 23. května 1978.

33 NA, A ÚV KSČ, fond 1261/0/7 (Předsednictvo ÚV KSČ 1976-1981), sv. 76, ar.j. 81, bod 2, Zpráva o oficiální přátelské návštěvě plk. Muamara Kaddáfího, generálního tajemníka Všeobecného lidového kongresu Libyjské arabské lidové socialistické džamáhírije, v Československé socialistické republice ve dnech 20. – 23.6.1978, 29. června 1978. NA, A ÚV KSČ, fond 1261/0/7 (Předsednictvo ÚV KSČ 1976-1981), sv. 80, ar.j. 83, bod 14, Zpráva o výsledcích jednání s vojenskou částí libyjské delegace o speciálních dodávkách, 24. srpna 1978. Baka, *Československá vojenská pomoc Líbyi v 70. rokoch 20. storočia*, p.63.

34 VÚA-VHA, MNO, 1980, karton 145, č.j. 07078-24/14-1977, Požadavek MZO na čs. vojenské piloty pro L-39 do Libye, listopad 1977. Fojtík, *Albatros*, pp.133–136.

35 Irra, *L-39 Albatros, 2. díl*, pp.29–32.

36 NA, A ÚV KSČ, fond 1261/0/7 (Předsednictvo ÚV KSČ 1976-1981), sv. 50, ar.j. 55, bod 7, Řešení pracovněprávních vztahů čs. odborníků vybraných pro zebezpečení technické pomoci Libyi, 28. září 1977.

37 VÚA-VHA, MNO, 1980, karton 145, č.j. 007078/4-14, dopis pro Gustáva Husáka, 27. října 1977. VÚA-VHA, MNO, 1980, karton 145, č.j. 0013553-84, 23. listopadu 1977. VÚA-VHA, MNO, 1980, karton 145, k č.j. 07078, Seznam zpráv. Václav Háva, Jak jsem pomáhal libyjské armádě - 2. díl, *Valka.cz*, https://www.valka.cz/Jak-jsem-pomahal-libyjske-armade-2-dil-t88653 (accessed 14 November 2020).

38 Irra, *L-39 Albatros, 2. díl*, pp.29–32.

39 VÚA-VHA, MNO, 1980, karton 145, k č.j. 7078, Přijetí československých odborníků v Libyi. VÚA-VHA, MNO, 1980, karton 145, č.j. 007078/36-14/1977, Přijetí čs. vojenských expertů k plnění úkolů technické pomoci Libyi podle usnesení PV ČSSR č. 136/1977, 17. listopadu 1977. VÚA-VHA, MNO, 1980, karton 145, k č.j. 007078/36-14/1977, Zpráva ze služební cesty pracovní skupiny, vedené plk. Matlasem ve dnech 26.10.-9.11.1977 v Libyi.

40 VÚA-VHA, MNO, 1980, karton 145, k č.j. 07078-45/14-1977, Autohavarie v Tripolisu 2.12.1977.

41 Václav Háva, Jak jsem pomáhal libyjské armádě - 1. díl, *Valka.cz*, https://www.valka.cz/Jak-jsem-pomahal-libyjske-armade-1-dil-t88652 (accessed 14 November 2020).

42 Václav Háva, Jak jsem pomáhal libyjské armádě - 2. díl, *Valka.cz*, https://www.valka.cz/Jak-jsem-pomahal-libyjske-armade-2-dil-t88653 (accessed 14 November 2020).

43 VÚA-VHA, MNO, 1980, karton 145, č.j. 007078/36-14/1977, Přijetí čs. expertů v Libyi.

44 Ibid.

45 VÚA-VHA, MNO, 1980, karton 140, č.j. 0373-79, Souhrnná zpráva o činnosti čs. vojenských odborníků za rok 1979, 30. prosince 1979. Baka, *Československá vojenská pomoc Líbyi v 70. rokoch 20. storočia*, p.67.

46 VÚA-VHA, MNO, 1980, karton 140, k č.j. 0495-80, Zaradenie čs. voj. odborníkov na kontrahované funkcie. VÚA-VHA, MNO, 1980, karton 140, k č.j. 102, Jmenný přehled odborníků /nových/ odesílaných 14.1.1981 do tank. skup.

47 VÚA-VHA, MNO, 1980, karton 140, č.j. 010038/37, Činnost čs. let. odborníků v rámci techn. pomoci Libyi, 24. ledna 1980.

48 VÚA-VHA, MNO, 1980, karton 140, č.j. 0373-79, Souhrnná zpráva o činnosti čs. vojenských odborníků za rok 1979, 30. prosince 1979. Irra, *L-39 Albatros, 3. díl*, p.11.

49 VÚA-VHA, MNO, 1980, karton 140, č.j. 010038/37, Činnost čs. let. odborníků v rámci techn. pomoci Libyi, 24. ledna 1980.

50 AMZV, TO-T 1975-1979, Libye, karton 5, obal 25, č.j. 01.152/79, Libyjské ozbrojené síly, 5. června 1979.

ABOUT THE AUTHOR

Martin Smisek was born in 1985 and received a master's degree in aerospace engineering at the Czech Technical University in Prague in 2010. In addition to his regular job of a mechanical design engineer, he has written over 70 articles about contemporary armoured vehicles, modern air-launched weapons as well as Czechoslovak military history and local conflicts since 1945. He is the author of the ground-breaking book *Super Sabry nad* Československem (Super Sabres over Czechoslovakia) about US spy flights over Czechoslovakia in 1955. Martin Smisek is also a regular contributor of the Czech and Slovak leading military website www.valka.cz.